HEALTHY LIVING

HEALTHY LIVING

volume

1

nutrition
personal care & hygiene
sexuality
physical fitness
environmental health

Caroline M. Levchuck
Michele Drohan
Jane Kelly Kosek

Allison McNeill, Editor

AN IMPRINT OF THE GALE GROUP

DETROIT · SAN FRANCISCO · LONDON
BOSTON · WOODBRIDGE, CT

Healthy Living

Caroline M. Levchuck, Michele Drohan, Jane Kelly Kosek

STAFF

Allison McNeill, *U•X•L Senior Editor*
Carol DeKane Nagel, *U•X•L Managing Editor*
Thomas L. Romig, *U•X•L Publisher*

Margaret A. Chamberlain, *Permissions Specialist (Pictures)*

Rita Wimberley, *Senior Buyer*
Evi Seoud, *Assistant Production Manager*
Dorothy Maki, *Manufacturing Manager*
Mary Beth Trimper, *Production Director*

Michelle DiMercurio, *Senior Art Director*
Cynthia Baldwin, *Product Design Manager*

Pamela Reed, *Imaging Coordinator*
Robert Duncan, *Imaging Specialist*
Randy Bassett, *Image Database Supervisor*
Barbara Yarrow, *Graphic Services Manager*

GGS Information Services, Inc., *Typesetting*

Cover illustration by Kevin Ewing Illustrations

Library of Congress Cataloging-in-Publication Data

Levchuck, Caroline M.
  Healthy living/Caroline Levchuck, Michele Drohan.
    p. cm.
  Contents: v. 1. Nutrition, exercise, and environmental health —v.2. Medicine and healthcare —v. 3. Mental health and self-esteem.
  Includes bibliographical references and index.
  ISBN 0-7876-3918-4 (set) —ISBN 0-7876-3919-2 (v.1) —ISBN 0-7876-3920-6 (v.2) —ISBN 0-7876-3921-4 (v.3)
  1. Health–Juvenile literature. 2. Mental health–Juvenile literature. 3. Medical care–Juvenile literature. [1. Health. 2. Mental health. 3. Medical care.] I. Drohan, Michele Ingber. II. Title.
RA777.L475 2000
613–dc21   99-053258

Contents

Reader's Guide

Healthy Living covers a wide range of health-related topics and lifestyle issues in fifteen chapters spread over three volumes. Each chapter is devoted to a specific health-related topic:

- Nutrition
- Personal Care and Hygiene
- Sexuality
- Physical Fitness
- Environmental Health
- Health Care Systems
- Health Care Careers
- Preventive Care
- Over-the-Counter Drugs
- Alternative Medicine
- Mental Health
- Mental Illness
- Eating Disorders
- Habits and Behaviors
- Mental Health Therapies

Each chapter begins with a brief overview to introduce readers to the topic at hand. Paired with the overview is a chapter-specific table of contents that outlines the main sections presented within the chapter.

A "Words to Know" box included at the beginning of each chapter provides definitions of words and terms used in that chapter. At the end of each chapter, under the heading "For More Information," appears a list of books and web sites that provides students with further information about that particular topic.

Health and safety tips, historical events, and other interesting facts relating to a particular topic are presented in sidebar boxes sprinkled throughout each chapter. More than 150 photos and illustrations enhance the text.

Each volume of *Healthy Living* includes a comprehensive glossary collected from all the "Words to Know" boxes in the fifteen chapters, and ends with a general bibliography section. The offerings in the bibliography provide more general health-related sources for further information. A cumulative index providing access to all major terms and topics covered throughout *Healthy Living* concludes each volume.

Related Reference Sources

Healthy Living is only one component of the three-part U•X•L Complete Health Resource. Other titles in this library include:

- *Sick! Diseases and Disorders, Injuries and Infections.* This four-volume set contains 140 alphabetically arranged entries on diseases, disorders, and injuries, including information on their causes, symptoms, diagnoses, tests and treatments, and prognoses. Each entry, four to seven pages long, includes sidebars on related people and topics, as well as a list of sources for further research. Each volume contains a 16-page color insert. *Sick* also features more than 240 black-and-white photographs and a cumulative subject index.
- *Body by Design: From the Digestive System to the Skeleton.* This two-volume set presents the anatomy (structure) and physiology (function) of the human body in twelve chapters. Each chapter is devoted to one of the eleven organ systems that make up the body. The last chapter focuses on the special senses, which allow humans to connect with the real world. Sidebar boxes present historical discoveries, recent medical advances, short biographies of scientists, and other interesting facts. More than 100 photos, many of them in color, illustrate the text. *Body by Design* also features a cumulative index.

Acknowledgements

A note of appreciation is extended to the *Healthy Living* advisors, who provided invaluable suggestions when this work was in its formative stages:

Carole Branson
Seminar Science Teacher
Wilson Middle School
San Diego, California

Bonnie L. Raasch
Media Specialist
Vernon Middle School
Marion, Iowa

Doris J. Ranke
Science Teacher
West Bloomfield High School
West Bloomfield, Michigan

Gracious thanks to Allison McNeill, Tom Romig, and Christine Slovey as well as the rest of the U•X•L team for their patience and first-rate editorial direction. Thanks also to Leslie Levchuck, R.D., Laura Wheeldreyer, Helen Packard, Stefanie Weiss, Kristin Ward, Lynda Beauregard, Robin Mayhall, Sean G. Levchuck, M.D., and Rosemarie Rich for their expertise and contributions to this project.

Comments and Suggestions

We welcome your comments on *Healthy Living*. Please write: Editors, *Healthy Living*, U•X•L, 27500 Drake Rd., Farmington Hills, Michigan, 48331–3535; call toll free: 1–800–877–4253; fax: 248–414–5043; or send e-mail via http://www.galegroup.com.

Please Read: Important Information

Healthy Living is a medical reference product designed to inform and educate readers about health and lifestyle issues. U•X•L believes this product to be comprehensive, but not necessarily definitive. While U•X•L has made substantial efforts to provide information that is accurate and up to date, U•X•L makes no representations or warranties of any kind, including without limitation, warranties of merchantability or fitness for a particular purpose, nor does it guarantee the accuracy, comprehensiveness, or timeliness of the information contained in this product.

Readers should be aware that the universe of medical knowledge is constantly growing and changing, and that differences of medical opinion exist among authorities. They are also advised to seek professional diagnosis and treatment for any medical condition, and to discuss information obtained from this book with their health care provider.

Words to Know

A

Abscess: When pus from a tooth infection spreads to the gums.

Abstinence: Voluntary, self-denial of sexual intercourse.

Accredit: To recognize an educational institution for having the standards that allows graduates to practice in a certain field.

Acetaminophen: A generic name for a compound that affects the brain and spinal cord, altering the perception of pain and lessening it.

Acid rain: Rain with a high content of sulfuric acid.

Acupuncture: A form of alternative medicine that involves stimulating certain points, referred to as acupoints, on a person's body to relieve pain and promote healing and overall well-being.

Adaptive behavior: Things a person does to adjust to new situations.

Addiction: The state of needing to compulsively repeat a behavior.

Adrenaline: A hormone that is released during times of high pressure, stress or fear; also a chemical that blocks the histamine response in an allergic reaction.

Advocate: A person who supports or defends a cause or a proposal.

Aerobic: Something that occurs in the presence of oxygen.

Affect: An individual's emotional response and demeanor.

Affectations: Artificial attitudes or behaviors.

Allergy: A chronic condition in which an allergic reaction occurs when the immune system responds aggressively to a certain foreign substance.

Allopath: A kind of doctor who advocates the conventional system of medical practice, which makes use of all measures that have proved to be effective in the treatment of disease.

Allopathic: The system of medical practice making use of all measures that have proved to be effective in the treatment of disease.

Altered consciousness: A state of awareness that is different from typical, waking consciousness; often induced with the use of drugs and alcohol.

Alternative medicine: Medical practices that fall outside the spectrum of conventional allopathic medicine.

Alzheimer's Disease: A degenerative disease of the brain that causes people to forget things, including thought, memory, language, and the people in their lives, and which eventually leads to death. Predominantly affects the elderly.

Amenorrhea: The absence of menstrual cycles.

Anaerobic: Something that occurs without oxygen because a person is using energy to do activities at a faster rate than the body is producing it.

Analgesic: A drug that alleviates pain without affecting consciousness.

Anemia: The condition of low iron in the blood.

Anhedonia: The inability to experience pleasure.

Anorexia nervosa: A term meaning "lack of appetite"; an eating disorder marked by a person's refusal to maintain a healthy body weight through restricting food intake or other means.

Antacids: A medication used to neutralize up to 99 percent of stomach acid.

Anti-inflammatory: Chemical that counteracts inflammation.

Antibiotics: Drugs used to treat bacterial infections.

Antibodies: A substance made in the body that protects the body against germs or viruses.

Antihistamine: The drugs most commonly used to treat allergies.

Antioxidants: Powerful molecules found in certain foods and vitamins that help neutralize free radicals, which are damaging molecules.

Antipsychotic drugs: Drugs that reduce psychotic behavior, often having negative long-term side-effects.

Antiseptic: A substance that prevents the growth of germs and bacteria.

Antitussive: A type of cough medication that calms the part of the brain that controls the coughing reflex.

Anus: An opening in the body through which solid waste is expelled.

Anxiety: An abnormal and overwhelming sense of worry and fear that is often accompanied by physical reaction.

Appeal: To take a court's decision and have another higher court review it to either uphold or overturn the first decision.

Archetypes: Universally known images or symbols that predispose an individual to have a specific feeling or thought about that image.

Aromatherapy: A branch of herbal medicine that uses medicinal properties found in the essential oils of certain plants.

Art therapy: The use of art forms and craft activities to treat emotional, mental and physical disabilities.

Arthritis: Chronic inflammation of the joints; the condition causes pain and swelling.

Artificial: Human-made; not found in nature.

Asbestos: A mineral fiber.

Associate's degree: Degree granted from two-year college institutions.

Astringent: Topical solution that tightens the skin.

Attention-Deficit/Hyperactivity Disorder (ADHD): A disorder that involves difficulty in concentrating and overall inattentiveness.

Autism: A developmental disorder marked by the inability to relate socially to others and by severe withdrawal from reality. Language limitations and the extreme desire for things to remain the same are common symptoms.

Autonomy: Being in charge of oneself; independent.

B

Bachelor's degree: A four-year college degree.

Bacteria: Single-celled micro-organisms, which can be either beneficial or harmful.

Bedside manner: A physician's ability to put a patient at ease and communicate effectively.

Behavior Therapy: A form of therapy that has its history in the experimental psychology and learning processes of humans and animals. Its main focus is to change certain behaviors instead of uncovering unconscious conflicts or problems.

Behavioral Medicine: Also known as health psychology, it is another developing mental health therapy technique in the field of medicine; the interdisciplinary study of ideas and knowledge taken from medicine and behavior science.

Behaviorism: Focuses on the study of observable behavior instead of on consciousness.

Benign: Harmless; also, non-cancerous.

Binge-eating disorder: An eating disorder that involves repetitive episodes of binge eating in a restricted period of time over several months.

Bingeing: When an individual eats, in a particular period of time, an abnormally large amount of food.

Bioenergetics: Body/mind therapy that stresses the body and the mind being freed of negative actions.

Biofeedback: The technique of making unconscious or involuntary bodily processes (as heartbeats or brain waves) perceptible in order to manipulate them by conscious mental control.

Bladder: An organ that holds urine.

Blood pressure: Pressure of blood against the walls of blood vessels.

Blood vessel: Vessel through which blood flows.

Body set-point theory: Theory of weight control that claims that the body will defend a certain weight regardless of factors such as calorie intake and exercise.

Bonding: Attaching a material to the surface of a tooth for cosmetic purposes.

Brief Therapy: Also called brief psychodynamic therapy, this form of therapy involves holding therapy sessions for a briefer period of time than the classic analytical form; brief therapy focuses on the specific situations that are causing patients upset

Bulimia nervosa: A term that means literally "ox hunger"; an eating disorder characterized by a repeated cycle of bingeing and purging.

Byproduct: Something other than the main product that is produced in a chemical or biological process.

C

Caffeine: An organic compound that has a stimulating effect on the central nervous system, heart, blood vessels, and kidneys.

Calcium: A mineral in the body that makes up much of the bones and teeth, helps nerve and muscle function, as well as the body's ability to convert food into energy.

Calorie: A unit of energy contained in the food and liquids that people consume.

Capitation: An agreement between doctor and managed health care organization wherein the doctor is paid per person.

Carbohydrate: The body's primary energy source, carbohydrates are the body's fuel.

Carbon monoxide: A highly toxic, colorless, odorless gas that is produced whenever something is burned incompletely or in a closed environment.

Carcinogenic: Cancer-causing.

Carcinogens: Substance that produces cancer.

Cardiovascular fitness: How efficiently the heart and lungs can pump blood (which holds oxygen) to muscles that are being worked.

Carve out: Medical services, such as substance abuse treatment, that are separated from the rest of the services within a health care plan.

Cervix: Narrow outer end of the uterus.

Chiropractic: A way of treating certain health conditions by manipulating and adjusting the spine.

Cholera: Any of several diseases of humans and domestic animals usually marked by severe gastrointestinal symptoms.

Cholesterol: A cousin to fat, is a steroid found only in foods that come from animals, such as egg yolks, organ meats, and cheese.

Chronic condition: A condition that lasts a long time or occurs frequently (e.g., asthma). Chronic conditions can be treated but not cured.

Circumcision: The removal of the foreskin from the glans of the penis.

Classical conditioning: Learning involving an automatic response to a certain stimulus that is acquired and reinforced through association.

Clinical trial: A study that evaluates how well a new drug works, positive effects, negative side effects, and how it is best used.

Clitoris: Small erectile organ in females at front part of the vulva.

Coexisting: Existing, or occurring, at the same time.

Cognition: The grouping of the mental processes of perception, recognition, conception, judgment, and reason.

Collagen: Fibrous protein found in connective tissues such as the skin and ligaments.

Collective unconscious: According to Karl Jung, the storage area for all the experiences that all people have had over the centuries. Also present in the collective unconscious are instincts, or strong motivations that are present from birth, and archetypes.

Compulsion: Habitual behaviors or mental acts an individual is driven to perform in order to reduce stress and anxiety brought on by obsessive thoughts.

Compulsive behavior: Behavior that is repeated over and over again, uncontrollably.

Conception: Also called fertilization. The formation of a cell capable of developing into a new being, such as when a man's sperm fertilizes a woman's egg creating a human embryo.

Congenital: Existing at birth.

Conscious: According to Karl Jung, the only level of which a person is directly aware.

Contaminate: To infect something or make something unsafe for use.

Continuing education: Formal schooling above and beyond any degree that is often required of medical professionals in order to keep practicing in their specific field.

Contraception: A birth control tool that prevents conception.

Convergent thinking: Thinking that is driven by knowledge and logic (opposite of divergent thinking).

Copayment: A fixed amount of money that patients pay for each doctor's visit and for each prescription.

Correlation: The relation of two or more things that is not naturally expected.

Cortisone: A hormone from the steroid family that originates in the adrenal cortex and is known for its antiinflammatory properties.

Cosmic: Relating to the universe in contrast to Earth.

Cowper's glands: Two small glands on either side of the male urethra, below the prostate gland, that produce a clear, sticky fluid that is thought to coat the urethra for passage of sperm.

Crash(ing): Coming down from being high on drugs or alcohol.

Creativity: One's capacity to think and solve problems in a unique way.

Credentials: Proof that a person is qualified to do a job.

Cruciform: The term for certain vegetables with long stems and branching tops, such as broccoli and cauliflower.

Cunnilingus: Oral stimulation of the female genitalia (vulva or clitoris).

Cut: The practice of mixing illegal drugs with another substance to produce a greater quantity of that substance.

Cuticle: The skin surrounding the nail.

D

Dance therapy: The use of dance and movement to treat or alleviate symptoms associated with mental or physical illness.

Date rape: Also called acquaintance rape; forced sexual intercourse between a person and someone she or he is acquainted with, is friends with, or is dating.

Decongestant: A compound that relieves a stuffy nose by limiting the production of mucus and reducing the swelling in the mucous membrane by constricting the blood vessels in the nose, opening the airways and promoting drainage.

Deductible: The amount of money a patient must pay for services covered by the insurance company before the plan will pay for any medical bills.

Defense mechanism: The ego's unconscious way of warding off a confrontation with anxiety.

Delirium: Mental disturbance marked by confusion, disordered speech, and even hallucinations.

Delusions: False, often illogical, beliefs that an individual holds in spite of proof that his or her beliefs are untrue.

Dependent: A reliance on something or someone.

Depression: Common psychological disorder characterized by intense and prolonged feelings of sadness, hopelessness, and irritability, as well as a lack of pleasure in activities.

Detoxification: The process of freeing an individual of an intoxicating or addictive substance in the body or to free from dependence.

Diagnostic: Used to recognize a disease or an illness.

Diarrhea: An increase in the frequency, volume, or wateriness of bowel movements.

Dissertation: An in-depth research paper.

Diuretic: A drug that expels water from the body through urination.

Divergent thinking: Thinking driven by creativity (opposite of convergent thinking).

Down syndrome: A form of mental retardation due to an extra chromosome present at birth, often accompanied by physical characteristics, such as sloped eyes.

Dream analysis: A technique of Freudian therapy that involves looking closely at a patient's dreams for symbolism and significance of themes and/or repressed thoughts.

Dysfunction: The inability to function properly.

Dyslexia: A reading disorder that centers on difficulties with word recognition.

E

Echinacea: A plant (also known as purple coneflower) that herbalists believe bolsters the immune system and treats certain ailments.

Edema: Swelling.

Ego: The part of one's personality that balances the drives of the id and the exterior world that is the center of the superego.

Eidetic memory: Also known as photographic memory; the ability to take a mental picture of information and use that picture later to retrieve the information.

Ejaculation: Sudden discharge of fluid (from penis).

Electrologist: A professional trained to perform electrolysis, or the removal of hair using electric currents.

Electromagnetic: Magnetism developed by a current of electricity.

Emergency: The unexpected onset of a serious medical condition or life-threatening injury that requires immediate attention.

Emission: Substances released into the air.

Empathy: Understanding of another's situation and feelings.

Emphysema: A chronic lung disease usually caused by smoking that produces shortness of breath and relentless coughing.

Enamel: The hard outer surface of the tooth.

Endocrine disrupter: Manmade chemical that looks and acts like a naturally-occurring hormone but which disturb the functioning of the naturally-occurring hormone.

Endometrial: Referring to mucous membrane lining the uterus.

Endorphin: Any of a group of natural proteins in the brain known as natural painkillers that make people feel good after exercising and act as the body's natural pain reliever.

Endurance: A person's ability to continue doing a stressful activity for an extended period of time.

Enema: A process that expels waste from the body by injecting liquid into the anus.

Enuresis: The inability to control one's bladder while sleeping at night; commonly known as bed-wetting.

Environmental tobacco smoke (ETS): The mixture of the smoke from a lit cigarette, pipe, or cigar and the smoke exhaled by the person smoking; commonly known as secondhand smoke or passive smoking.

Enzyme: A complex protein found in the cells that acts as a catalyst for chemical reactions in the body.

Ephedra: A type of plant (also known as Ma Huang) used to treat ailments, including bronchial problems, and as a decongestant.

Epidemic: The rapid spreading of a disease to many people at the same time.

Epidemiology: The study of disease in a population.

Epididymis: System of ducts leading from the testes that holds sperm.

Esophagus: The muscular tube that connects the throat with the stomach.

Estrogen: Hormone that stimulates female secondary sex characteristics.

Euphoric: Having the feeling of well-being or elation (extreme happiness).

Exercise: A subset of physical activity, which is an activity that is structured and planned.

Exercise addiction: Also known as compulsive exercise, a condition in which participation in exercise activities is taken to an extreme; an individual exercises to the detriment of all other things in his or her life.

Existential therapy: Therapy that stresses the importance of existence and urges patients to take responsibility for their psychological existence and well-being.

Expectorant: A type of cough medication that helps clear the lungs and chest of phlegm.

Extrovert: Being outgoing and social.

F

Fallopian tubes: Pair of tubes that conducts the egg from the ovary to the uterus .

Fat: Part of every cell membrane and the most concentrated source of energy in one's diet, fat is used by the body to insulate, cushion, and support vital organs.

Fee-for-service: When a doctor or hospital is paid for each service performed.

Fellatio: Oral stimulation of the male genitalia.

Fellowship: Advanced study and research that usually follows a medical residency.

Feverfew: An herb used to treat migraines.

Fluoride: A chemical compound that is added to toothpaste and drinking water to help prevent tooth decay.

Formulary: A list of prescription drugs preferred by a health plan for its members.

Free radicals: Harmful molecules in the body that damage normal cells and can cause cancer and other disorders.

Fungus: An organism of plant origin that lacks chlorophyll; some fungi cause irritation or disease (a mold is a kind of fungus).

G

Gallstone: Stones made up of cholesterol or calcium that form in the gall-bladder.

Generic drug: A drug that is approved by the Food and Drug Administration but does not go by a specific brand name and therefore is less expensive than a brand name drug.

Genetic: Something present in the genes that is inherited from a person's biological parents; hereditary.

Genetic predisposition: To be susceptible to something because of genes.

Genitalia: The reproductive organs.

Geriatric: Elderly.

Gestalt therapy: A humanistic therapy that urges individuals to satisfy growing needs, acknowledge previously unexpressed feelings, and reclaim facets of their personalities that have been denied.

Gingivitis: An inflammation of the gums that is the first stage of gum disease.

Ginkgo biloba: A tree (the oldest living kind of tree, in fact) whose leaves are believed to have medicinal value, particularly in aiding memory and treating dizziness, headaches, and even anxiety.

Ginseng: An herb used as a kind of cureall, with benefits to the immune system and aiding the body in coping with stress. Some also believe it aids concentration.

Gland: A part of the body that makes a fluid that is either used or excreted by the body; glands make sweat and bile.

H

Habit: A behavior or routine that is repeated.

Halitosis: Chronic bad breath caused by poor oral hygiene, illness, or another condition.

Hallucination: The illusion of seeing or hearing something that does not really exist; can occur because of nervous system disorders or in response to drugs.

Hangnail: Loose skin near the base of the nail.

Hangover: The syndrome that occurs after being high on drugs or drinking alcohol, often including nausea, headache, dizziness, and fuzzy-mindedness.

Health Maintenance Organization (HMO): A health plan that generally covers preventive care, such as yearly checkups and immunizations. Care must be provided by a primary care physician and services must be approved by the plan in order to be covered.

Heart disease: When arteries become clogged with a fatty buildup; this can cause a heart attack or a stroke.

Heat stroke: A serious condition that causes the body to stop sweating and overheat dangerously.

Hemoglobin: A protein found in red blood cells, needed to carry oxygen to the body's many tissues.

Hemorrhoids: A form of varicose veins that occurs when the veins around the anus become swollen or irritated.

Hepatitis: One of several severe liver-damaging diseases specified by the letters A, B, C and D.

Herbicide: A chemical agent used to kill damaging plants, such as weeds.

Histamines: Chemicals released in an allergic reaction that cause swelling of body tissues.

Holistic: Of or relating to the whole rather than its parts; holistic medicine tries to treat both the mind and the body.

Homeopathy: A kind of alternative medicine that employs natural remedies.

Hormone: Substances found in the body's glands that control some of the body's functions, such as growth.

Humane: Marked by compassion or sympathy for other people or creatures.

Humanistic: A philosophy that places importance on human interests and dignity, stressing the individual over the religious or spiritual.

Hymen: Fold of mucous membrane partly closing the orifice of the vagina.

Hypertension: High blood pressure.

Hypnosis: A trance-like state of consciousness brought about by suggestions of relaxation, which is marked by increased suggestibility.

Hypoallergenic: Unlikely to cause an allergic reaction.

Hypothesize: To make a tentative assumption or educated guess in order to draw out and test its logical or observable consequences.

I

Ibuprofen: The generic name for a type of analgesic that works in the same manner as aspirin but can be used in instances when aspirin cannot.

Id: According to Sigmund Freud, the biological instincts that revolve around pleasure, especially sexual and aggressive impulses.

Identical twins: Also called monozygotic twins; twins born from the same egg and sperm.

Immune system: The body's own natural defenses against germs and other infectious agents; protects the body against illness.

Immunization: The introduction of disease-causing compounds into the body in very small amounts in order to allow the body to form antigens against the disease.

Incinerator: A machine that burns waste materials.

Indemnity plan: A plan in which the insurance company sets a standard amount that it will pay for specific medical services.

Indigenous: Occurring naturally in an environment.

Industrial: Relating to a company that manufactures a product.

Inert: A chemical agent lacking in active properties.

Infection: A disease that is caused by bacteria.

Infinitesimals: Immeasurably small quantity or variable.

Inhalants: Substances that people sniff to get high.

Inherent: Belonging to the essential nature of something.

Innate: Inborn; something (a characteristic) a person is born with.

Insight therapy: A group of different therapy techniques that assume that a person's behavior, thoughts, and emotions become disordered as a result of the individual's lack of understanding as to what motivates him or her.

Insomnia: Chronic sleeplessness or sleep disturbances.

Insulin: The substance in the body that regulates blood sugar levels.

Intelligence: The ability and capacity to understand.

Intelligence Quotient (IQ): A standardized measure of a person's mental ability as compared to those in his or her age group.

Interaction: When two drugs influence the effects of each other.

Internalized: To incorporate something into one's self.

Internship: Supervised practical experience.

Intestinal: Having to do with the intestine, the part of the body that digests food.

Introvert: Being quiet and soft-spoken.

Iridology: The study of the iris of the eye in order to diagnose illness or disease.

Iron-deficiency anemia: When the body is lacking in the right amount of red blood cells, caused by a deficiency of iron.

Irrational: Lacking reason or understanding.

K

Keratin: A tough protein produced by the body that forms the hair and nails.

Kidney stone: Stones made of calcium or other minerals that form in the kidney or the ureter, which leads to the bladder.

Kinesiology: The study of anatomy in relation to movement of the body.

Kleptomania: Habitual stealing or shoplifting.

L

Labia majora: Outer fatty folds of the vulva (big lips).

Labia minora: Inner connective folds of the vulva (little lips).

Lanugo: Fine hair that grows all over the body to keep it warm when the body lacks enough fat to accomplish this.

Larynx: The voice box.

Laxatives: Drugs that induces bowel movements and alleviate constipation, or the inability to have a bowel movement.

Leaching: The process of dissolving outward by the action of a permeable substance.

Lead: A heavy, flexible, metallic element that is often used in pipes and batteries.

Learning: Modifying behavior and acquiring new information or skills.

Learning disorders: Developmental problems relating to speech, academic, or language skills that are not linked to a physical disorder or mental retardation.

Licensed: Authorization to practice a certain occupation.

M

Mantra: A phrase repeated during meditation to center the mind.

Manual: Involving the hands.

Massage therapy: The manipulation of soft tissue in the body with the aim of relieving and preventing pain, stress, and muscle spasms.

Master's degree: A college degree that ranks above a four-year bachelor's degree.

Masturbation: Erotic stimulation of one's own genitals.

Maturation: Process of becoming mature; developing, growing up.

Medicaid: The joint state-federal health care program for low-income people.

Medicare: The federal health insurance program for senior citizens.

Medigap: Private insurance that helps pay for some of the costs involved in Medicare.

Meditation: The act of focusing on one's own thoughts for the purpose of relaxation.

Memory: The ability to acquire, store, and retrieve information.

Menstruation: Monthly discharge of blood and tissue debris from the uterus.

Metabolism: The rate at which the body uses energy.

Microscopic: Invisible without the use of a microscope, an instrument that enlarges images of tiny objects.

Mineral: A nutrient that helps regulate cell function and provides structure for cells.

Modeling: Learning based on modeling one's behavior on that of another person with whom an individual strongly identifies.

Monosodium glutamate (MSG): A substance that enhances flavor but causes food intolerance in some people.

Mortality: The number of deaths in a given time or place.

Mucous membranes: The lining of the nose and sinus passages that helps shield the body from allergens and germs.

Mucus: A slippery secretion that is produced by mucous membranes, which it moistens and protects.

Musculoskeletal: Relating to the muscles and bones.

Music therapy: The use of music to treat or alleviate symptoms associated with certain mental or physical illnesses.

N

National health care system: A system in which the government provides medical care to all its citizens.

Nature: The biological or genetic makeup of a person.

Naturopathy: A kind of alternative medicine that focuses on the body's inherent healing powers and works with those powers to restore and maintain overall health.

Neurons: Nerve cells that receive chemical-electrical impulses from the brain.

Neurosis: An emotional disorder that produces fear and anxiety.

Neurotransmitters: A substance that transmits nerve impulses.

Nicotine: An organic compound in tobacco leaves that has addictive properties.

Nitrogen dioxide: A gas that cannot be seen or smelled. It irritates the eyes, ears, nose, and throat.

Noninvasive: Not involving penetration of the skin.

Nonproductive cough: A dry and hacking cough.

Nurture: How a person is raised, by whom, and in what environment.

Nutrient: Food substances that nourish the body.

O

Obesity: The condition of being very overweight.

Observational learning: Learning by observing the behavior of others.

Obsessions: Repeating thoughts, impulses, or mental images that are irrational and which an individual cannot control.

Off-label drug: A drug that is not formally approved by the Food and Drug Administration but is approved for legal use in some medical treatments.

Operant conditioning: Learning involving voluntary response to a certain stimuli based on positive or negative consequences resulting from the response.

Oral sex: Sexual activity involving the mouth.

Organic: Occurring naturally.

Orgasm: The peak or climax of sexual excitment.

Osteopathy: A system of medical practice based on the theory that disease is due chiefly to mechanical misalignment of bones or body parts.

Osteoporosis: A degenerative bone disease involving a decrease in bone mass, making bones more fragile.

Ova: Female reproductive cells; also called eggs.

Ovaries: Female reproductive organs that produce eggs and female sex hormones.

Overdose: A dangerous, often deadly, reaction to taking too much of a certain drug.

Ovulation: Discharge of mature ovum from the ovary.

Ozone layer: The atmospheric shield that protects the planet from harmful ultraviolet radiation.

P

Palpitation: Rapid, irregular heartbeat.

Panacea: A cure-all.

Parasites: Any plant or animal that lives on or in another plant or animal and gets food from it at the expense of its host.

Parkinson's disease: A progressive disease that causes slowing and stiffening of muscular activity, trembling hands, and a difficulty in speaking and walking.

Particle: A microscopic pollutant released when fuel does not burn completely.

Penis: Male sex organ and channel by which urine and ejaculate leave the body.

Perception: One's consciousness and way of observing things.

Periodontal disease: Gum disease, the first stage of which is gingivitis.

Person-Centered Therapy: A form of therapy put forth by Carl Rogers that looks at assumptions made about human nature and how we can try to understand them. It posits that people should be responsible for themselves, even when they are troubled.

Personal unconscious: According to Karl Jung, the landing area of the brain for the thoughts, feelings, experiences, and perceptions that are not picked up by the ego.

Personality: All the traits and characteristics that make people unique.

Pesticide: A chemical agent used to kill insects and other pests.

Pharmacotherapy: The use of medication to treat emotional and mental problems.

Phenylpropanolamine (PPA): A chemical that disrupts the hunger signals being sent by the brain; it is often used in weight loss aids.

Phlegm: Sticky mucus present in the nose, throat, and lungs.

Phobia: A form of an anxiety disorder that involves intense and illogical fear of an object or situation.

Physical activity: Any movement that spends energy.

Physiological: Relating to the functions and activities of life on a biological level.

Physiology: A branch of science that focuses on the functions of the body.

Pinna: Outer part of the ear; part of the ear that is visible.

Plaque: A sticky film of bacteria that grows around the teeth.

Plaster: A medicated or protective dressing that consists of a film (as of cloth or plastic) usually spread with a medicated substance.

Point of service (POS): A health plan in which members can see the doctor of their choosing at the time they need to see a doctor.

Pores: Small openings in the skin.

Post-Traumatic Stress Disorder (PTSD): Reliving trauma and anxiety related to an event that occurred earlier.

Potassium: A chemical element that is a silver-white, soft metal occurring in nature.

Predisposition: To be susceptible to something.

Preferred provider organization (PPO): A health plan in which members have their health care paid for only when they choose from a network of doctors and hospitals.

Premium: Fee paid for a contract of insurance.

Preventive care: Medical care that helps to maintain one's health, such as regular checkups.

Primary care physician: The doctor who is responsible for the total care of a patient and has the ability to refer patients to other doctors or specialists.

Pro-choice: Supports a woman's choice in regard to abortion.

Productive cough: A cough that brings up phlegm.

Prohibition: An era in the 1920s when alcohol was made illegal.

Prostaglandin: A hormonelike substance that affects blood vessels and the functions of blood platelets, and sensitizes nerve endings to pain.

Prostate gland: A muscular glandular body situated at the base of the male urethra.

Protein: An organic substance made of amino acids that are necessary for human life.

Protozoan: One-celled organism that can cause disease in humans.

Psychiatry: The branch of medicine that relates to the study and treatment of mental illness.

Psychoactive: Something that affects brain function, mood and behavior.

Psychoanalysis: A theory of psychotherapy, based on the work of Sigmund Freud, involving dream analysis, free association, and different facets of the self (id, ego, superego).

Psychodrama: A therapy that involves a patient enacting or reenacting life situations in order to gain insight and alter behavior. The patient is the actor while the therapist is the director.

Psychodynamics: The forces (emotional and mental) that develop in early childhood and how they affect behavior and mental well-being.

Psychological vulnerability: Used to describe individuals who are potential candidates for drug addiction because of prior experiences or other influences.

Psychology: The scientific study of mental processes and behaviors.

Psychophysical energy: Energy made up of energy from the body and the mind.

Psychotherapy: The general term of an interaction in which a trained mental health professional tries to help a patient resolve emotional and mental distress.

Puberty: The onset of sexual maturation in young adults; usually between the ages of 13 and 16 in males and 12 and 15 in females.

Purging: When a person gets rid of the food that she has eaten by vomiting, taking an excessive amount of laxatives, diuretics, or enemas or engaging in fasting and/or excessive exercise.

Pyromania: Habitual need to start fires.

Q

Qi (or Chi): Life energy vital to an individual's well-being.

R

Radiation: Energy or rays emitted when certain changes occur in the atoms or molecules of an object or substance.

Radon: A colorless, odorless, radioactive gas produced by the naturally occurring breakdown of the chemical element uranium in soil or rocks.

RapidEye Movement (REM) sleep: A deep stage of sleep during which time people dream.

Rational-emotive behavior therapy: Therapy that seeks to identify a patient's irrational beliefs as the key to changing behavior rather than examining the cause of the conflict itself.

Rationing: The process of limiting certain products or services because of a shortage.

Reality therapy: A therapy that empowers people to make choices and control their own destinies.

Referral: Permission from the primary care physician to see another doctor.

Reflexology: A type of alternative medicine that involves applying pressure to certain points, referred to as reflex points, on the foot.

Registered: To complete the standards of education issued by a state government to practice a certain profession.

Rehabilitation: To restore or improve a condition of health or useful activity.

Reimbursement plan: A plan where a patient must pay for medical services up front and then get paid back from the insurance company.

Reinforcement: Making something stronger by adding extra support.

Remorse: Ill feelings stemming from guilt over past actions.

Residency: Advanced training in a medical specialty that includes or follows a physician's internship.

Residential treatment: Treatment that takes place in a facility in which patients reside.

Right-to-life: Supports anti-abortion (with possible exceptions for incest and rape) movement.

Ritual: Observances or ceremonies that mark change, renewal, or other events.

Russell's sign: Calluses, cuts, and sores on the knuckles from repeated self-induced vomiting.

S

St. John's Wort: An herb used as an antiinflammatory drug, to treat depression, and as an analgesic.

Saturated fat: Fat that is solid at room temperature.

Savant: A person with extensive knowledge in a very specific area.

Schizophrenia: A chronic psychological disorder marked by scattered, disorganized thoughts, confusion, and delusions.

Scrotum: External pouch that contains the testes.

Sebum: An oily substance that lubricates the hair shaft.

Secondhand smoke: Also known as environmental tobacco smoke (ETS). The mixture of the smoke from a lit cigarette, pipe, or cigar and the smoke exhaled by the person smoking.

Sectarian medicine: Medical practices not based on scientific experience; also known as alternative medicine.

Self-esteem: How an individual feels about her or himself.

Self-medicate: When a person treats an ailment, mental or physical, with alcohol or drugs rather than seeing a physician or mental health professional.

Sexual abuse: All levels of sexual contact against anyone's will, including inappropriate touching, kissing, and intercourse.

Sexual harassment: All unwanted and unsolicited sexual advances, talk, and behavior.

Sexual intercourse: Involves genital contact between individuals.

Side effect: A secondary (and usually negative) reaction to a drug.

Smegma: Cheesy sebaceous matter that collects between the penis and the foreskin.

Social Security: A government program that provides economic security to senior citizens and the disabled.

Social norms: Things that are standard practices for the larger part of society.

Somatogenesis: Having origins from within the body, as opposed to the mind.

Specialist: A doctor who concentrates on only one area of medicine, such as a dermatologist (skin specialist).

Specialize: To work in a special branch of a certain profession.

Sperm: Male reproductive cell.

Sterilization: A process that makes something free of living bacteria.

Stimulant: Substance that excites the nervous system and may produce a temporary increase in ability.

Stimulus: Something that causes action or activity.

Stressor: Something (for example, an event) that causes stress.

Stroke: A sudden loss of consciousness, feeling, and voluntary movement caused by a blood clot in the brain.

Subatomic: Relating to particles smaller than atoms.

Suicide: Taking one's own life.

Sulfur dioxide: A toxic gas that can also be converted to a colorless liquid.

Superego: According to Sigmund Freud, the part of one's personality that is concerned with social values and rules.

Suppress: To stop the development or growth of something.

Symptom: Something that indicates the presence of an illness or bodily disorder.

Synapse: Gaps between nerves; the connections between neurons that allow people to make mental connections.

Synthetic: Human-made; not found in nature.

T

Temperament: How a person behaves.

Tendinitis: Inflammation of a tendon.

Testicles: Male reproductive gland that produces sperm.

Testosterone: Hormone produced by testes.

Thyroid: A gland that controls the growth of the body

Tic: A quirk of behavior or speech that happens frequently.

Tolerance: The build-up of resistance to the effects of a substance.

Topical: Designed for application on the body.

Tourette's Disorder: A disorder marked by the presence of multiple motor tics and at least one vocal tic, as well as compulsions and hyperactivity.

Toxic: Relating to or caused by a poison

Toxins: Poisonous substances.

Transference: A patient's responses to an analyst that are not in keeping with the analyst-patient relationship but seem instead to resemble ways of behaving toward significant people in the patient's past.

Transient: Passes quickly into and out of existence.

U

Ultrasound: The use of high-frequency sound waves that forms an image to detect a problem in the body.

Unsaturated fat: Fat that is liquid at room temperature, like vegetable oil.

Uranium: A chemical element that is a silver-white, hard metal and is radioactive.

Urethra: The tube from the bladder to outside the body through which urine is expelled.

Uterus: Womb; female organ that contains and nourishes an embryo/fetus.

V

Vaccine: A substance made up of weak bacteria and put into the body to help prevent disease.

Vagina: The female canal that leads from the cervix (or opening of the uterus) to the vulva (or the external female genitalia).

Vas deferens: Spermatic duct connected to the epididymis and seminal vesicle.

Vasoconstrictor: A drug that constricts the blood vessels to affect the blood pressure.

Vegan: A strict vegetarian who doesn't eat any animal by-products or any dairy.

Vegetarian: A person who lives on a diet free of meat products; some vegetarians will eat eggs or dairy products, while others will not.

Veneer: A covering, often made of porcelain, that is placed over a tooth that is damaged or for cosmetic reasons.

Vertebra: A bony piece of the spinal column fitting together with other vertebrae to allow flexible movement of the body. (The spinal cord runs through the middle of each vertebra.)

Virus: A tiny organism that causes disease.

Vitamin: A nutrient that enables the body to use fat, protein, and carbohydrates effectively.

Volatile organic compound (VOC): An airborne chemical that contains carbon.

W

Withdrawal: The phase of removal of drugs or alcohol from the system of the user.

Y

Yeast infection: A common infection of a woman's vagina caused by overgrowth of the yeast Candida Albicans.

Yoga: A form of exercise and a system of health that involves yoga postures to promote well-being of body and mind through regulated breathing, concentration, and flexibility.

HEALTHY LIVING

1

Nutrition

Nutrition refers to the manner in which the body makes use of food. It not only includes eating the correct amounts and kinds of foods, but also the processes by which the body uses food substances for growth, repair, and maintenance of body activities. Nutrition also concerns the role that food plays in our lives and the many factors that determine our food choices.

Good nutrition during adolescence is very important for the achievement of full growth potential and optimal health as well as for the prevention of certain adult chronic (frequently recurring) diseases. Poor eating habits formed during childhood and the teen years may, in combination with other factors, increase the risk for chronic diseases later in life such as heart disease, osteoporosis (a disease that causes bones to become fragile), and some forms of cancer. Eating habits also affect the risk for immediate health problems including iron deficiency anemia (a blood disease), high blood pressure, and tooth decay.

Food is basic to survival, and people have built-in mechanisms in their bodies that work to control how much they eat, when they eat, and what they eat. In addition to these built-in mechanisms, there are many other factors that affect the way people eat. What, when, and how much people eat is greatly influenced by emotional, social, cultural, and economic factors. However, eating too much, too little, or not eating some of each type of food can make people unhealthy.

Good nutrition is a complex issue that not only has immediate benefits but also is an investment in a person's future health. Adolescence is a critical period for establishing the foundation for healthful eating patterns.

EATING WELL: WHY IT'S IMPORTANT

Throughout history humans have written about food and its effect on the body. In recent years people have learned more and more about nutrition through laboratory studies conducted on animals and humans. The role of nutrition in health and disease has been recognized from research as early as 1900, although much remains to be learned.

By choosing healthy eating habits, people will gain many rewards. Eating healthy foods helps people maintain a healthy weight while also providing them with plenty of energy. Not only will people feel better and have more energy when eating well, but their skin, teeth, and hair will also reflect their good choices. The choices people make now can also affect their health later in life. People's risk for developing major health problems such as heart

WORDS TO KNOW

Body set-point theory: The set point theory of weight control holds that the body will defend a certain weight regardless of external factors, such as calorie intake or exercise.

Calcium: A mineral in the body that makes up much of the bones and teeth, helps nerve and muscle function, as well as the body's ability to convert food into energy.

Calorie: A unit of energy contained in the food and liquids that people consume.

Carbohydrate: The body's primary energy source, carbohydrates are the body's fuel.

Cholesterol: A cousin to fat, is a steroid found only in foods that come from animals, such as egg yolks, organ meats, and cheese.

Chronic disease: An illness that is present for a long time. A frequently recurring disease, such as asthma.

Enzyme: Protein molecules that further chemical reactions in the body.

Fat: Part of every cell membrane and the most concentrated source of energy in one's diet, fat is used by the body to insulate, cushion, and support vital organs.

Gallstone: Stones made up of cholesterol or calcium that form in the gallbladder.

Heart disease: When arteries become clogged with a fatty buildup; this can cause a heart attack or a stroke.

Hormone: Substances found in the body's glands that control some of the body's functions, such as growth.

Iron-deficiency anemia: When the body is lacking in the right amount of red blood cells, caused by a deficiency of iron.

Kidney stone: Stones made of calcium or other minerals that form in the kidney or the ureter, which leads to the bladder.

Metabolism: The rate at which the body uses energy.

Mineral: A nutrient that helps regulate cell function and provides structure for cells.

Nutrient: Food substances that nourish the body.

Obesity: A condition marked by too much body fat.

Osteoporosis: A disease that causes bones to become fragile.

Protein: An organic substance made of amino acids that are necessary for human life.

Saturated fat: Fat that is solid at room temperature.

Unsaturated fat: Fat that is liquid at room temperature, like vegetable oil.

Vegan: A strict vegetarian who doesn't eat any animal by-products or any dairy.

Vegetarian: A person who lives on a diet free of meat products; some vegetarians will eat eggs or dairy products, while others will not.

Vitamin: A nutrient that enables the body to use fat, protein, and carbohydrates effectively.

disease, stroke, diabetes, and cancer can be reduced if they make the right food choices a part of their lives. Good nutrition will help people to look and feel their best today and help prevent some of the deadliest health problems in the future. An unhealthy diet, lack of regular physical activity, smoking, and the over-consumption of alcohol are the leading contributors to premature death in the United States. It's important to eat well—good nutrition can save lives.

To better understand the diet link in health and disease, government agencies continue to study nutrition. Many controversies remain and a lot still needs to be explained; however, general guidelines have been developed to illustrate what Americans can do through proper diet to ensure good health.

Nutrients

Just as a car needs gasoline, a form of fuel, to run, people need food for fuel every day. Food is the source of all nutrients needed for life. Nutrients are substances used by the body for fuel, growth, and all body processes. The body needs more than fifty different nutrients every day to maintain proper health. Nutrient needs are higher in adolescence than any other time in the life cycle because the body is experiencing its biggest growth spurt at this time.

The nutrients people get from food are vitamins, minerals, carbohydrates, fats, protein, and water. People's bodies need all of these nutrients to remain healthy. Calories people eat come from fat, carbohydrates, and protein. Fat, carbohydrates, and protein are essential nutrients, which means people need them for good health. Vitamins and minerals are necessary for good health but have no calories. The body depends on good food choices to get all of these nutrients in the right amounts every day.

FAT. Fat provides the most concentrated source of energy in our diet. It also provides flavor and texture to foods. Fat in the body functions to insulate, cushion, and support vital organs and is a part of every cell membrane. Fat in our diet mainly comes from fatty meats, whole milk and whole milk dairy products (such as yogurt), butter, and baked goods. Fat can be saturated (solid at room temperature) or unsaturated (liquid at room temperature).

CARBOHYDRATES. Carbohydrates are the fuel the body needs to function. The brain primarily uses carbohydrates as its energy source. Most carbohydrates are plant-based from grains, fruits, and vegetables. There are three types of carbohydrates: sugar, starch, and fiber.

PROTEIN. Proteins act as the building blocks of the body. The body uses protein to make and maintain body tissue such as muscles and organs. It also functions as the key component of enzymes and hormones. Milk, eggs, cheese, meat, and fish are the most common sources of protein, although beans and nuts are good sources as well.

VITAMINS. Vitamins are needed in the right amounts by the body for normal growth, digestion, mental alertness, and resistance to infections. They enable the body to use fat, protein, and carbohydrates. There are thirteen different vitamins, four of which are stored in fat.

MINERALS. Like vitamins, minerals are needed in small amounts by the body. They help regulate cell function and provide structure for cells. There are fifteen minerals needed by the body; the most common ones are calcium, phosphorous, and magnesium.

WATER. Next to oxygen, water is most important to life. A person's body is 50 to 70 percent water. Although people can live for weeks without food, they can exist for only a few days without water. People need eight to ten cups of water each day.

Calories

Calories are units of energy contained in the foods people eat. The amount of calories a food has reflects how much energy it supplies to the body. The more calories a food has, the more energy it contains. The body needs energy to do everything from breathing and pumping blood to walking and running. If people eat more calories than their body burns, their body stores the excess energy as body fat.

Only the nutrients fat, protein, and carbohydrates contain calories and therefore provide energy. Vitamins and minerals don't actually supply calo-

DIETARY GUIDELINES FOR AMERICANS

The Dietary Guidelines for Americans take into account all of the currently known information about nutrition as well as the various controversies. These guidelines were issued jointly by the United States Department of Agriculture and the United States Department of Health and Human Services in 1995. The guidelines contain general health suggestions and dietary recommendations to help promote and maintain wellness.

These dietary guidelines give people direction in making better food choices to improve their health but they don't answer all of the questions of how to eat a more healthful diet. The Food Guide Pyramid was created to help better explain how to achieve the dietary guidelines.

Dietary Guidelines for Americans

Eat a variety of foods. It is important to eat a variety of foods from the different food groups each day. No two foods contain exactly the same nutrients in the same amounts. Varying the types of fruits, vegetables, grains, milk, or protein foods eaten each day helps people get all of the important nutrients their body requires.

Balance good nutrition with physical activity. Being an active person is just as important as eating healthful foods. Inactivity and poor nutrition are the leading risk factors associated with health problems later in life such as heart disease, high blood pressure, and diabetes. Being underweight can also pose serious health risks because it can mean the body isn't getting the essential nutrients it needs.

Choose a diet low in fat, saturated fat, and cholesterol. Eating a lot of foods high in saturated fat

ries but are vital in the processing of the energy-producing nutrients. Fat provides the most energy—nine calories per gram. Protein and carbohydrate both provide four calories per gram. A gram is roughly the same weight as a paper clip.

THE FOOD GUIDE PYRAMID

Adolescents need a practical guide to help them make food choices to meet their nutritional needs. During the twentieth century and especially in recent years, several food guides have been developed by a number of government agencies. Currently, the Food Guide Pyramid is the most widely accepted food guide that incorporates the recommendations of the Dietary Guidelines for Americans.

The Food Guide Pyramid was created to help Americans choose a healthful diet. The guide addresses two main dietary problems: diet excesses and diet deficiencies. Several of the major causes of death in the United States are linked to diets that contain too much fat, saturated fat, cholesterol, or sodium. On the other hand, bodies need enough protein, vitamins, minerals, and fiber to grow and stay healthy. People who eat too many foods with a lot of calories but few or no nutrients, like soft drinks and candy, can develop nutrient deficiencies.

(fat that is solid at room temperature) can lead to the clogging of arteries, which can begin in the childhood years. When arteries become clogged with a fatty buildup, it is called heart disease. Heart disease can lead to a heart attack or stroke, two of the leading causes of premature death in the United States.

Choose a diet with plenty of grain products, vegetables, and fruits. Most grain foods, vegetables, and fruits are naturally low in fat and are packed with vitamins, minerals, and carbohydrates. Whole grain products, fruits, and vegetables also contain fiber, a nutrient important for good digestive health. A healthy diet is one that is based on these three food groups.

Choose a diet moderate in sugars. Filling up on sugary foods leaves less room for healthier foods with more vitamins and minerals. Foods high in sugar are often also high in fat and have been shown to cause tooth decay.

Choose a diet moderate in salt and sodium. Most people eat more salt than is needed. Excess salt in the diet has been shown to contribute to high blood pressure in people at a high risk for developing high blood pressure.

If you drink alcoholic beverages, do so in moderation. [Consumption of alcoholic beverages by minors is illegal and NOT recommended for children or teenagers under any circumstances.] Alcohol provides calories but few or no nutrients, can alter judgement, and can lead to a dependency or addiction. For adults, it is recommended that alcohol be consumed in moderate amounts.

The food pyramid depicts six food categories and emphasizes that the American diet should include greater amounts of grain foods, fruits and vegetables, and lesser amounts of fats and sugars. Its shape is very important to its message, as it visually represents how much food people need from each of the six categories. Each group is equally important, but people need foods from the bottom in larger amounts than foods closer to the top of the pyramid. The food pyramid emphasizes the following key points:

- Eat a variety of foods every day.
- Choose foods with less fat and sugar.
- Eat plenty of whole grain foods, fruits and vegetables (preferably raw).

While the food pyramid divides foods into six categories, there are five major food groups. The food category at the tip of the pyramid is not considered a major food group since these foods should be used sparingly for good health. The food pyramid reminds people to eat a variety of foods to get all of the nutrients they need as well as the right amount of food to main-

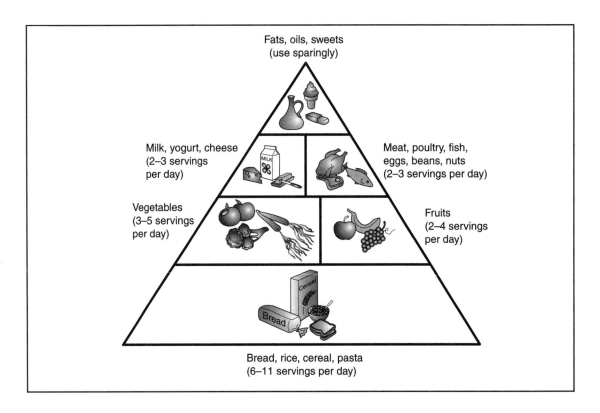

The Food Guide Pyramid shows how many servings from each food group an individual should have each day. (Electronic Illustrators Group. Reproduced by permission of Gale Group.)

tain a healthy weight. The foods are grouped together according to the key nutrients they provide. Foods provide many more nutrients besides their key nutrients but by eating plenty of foods with key nutrients, people are more likely to get the correct balance of all nutrients.

The food pyramid also provides information on how much to eat from each group. It recommends a range of servings needed each day from each of the major food groups. The amount of calories and key nutrients people need determines how many servings they should have. A serving is a specific amount of food, which is different for each food category. The amount of calories or energy people need depends on how old they are, how active they are, and how much they weigh.

In general, boys need more energy than most girls and therefore more servings. This is due to the fact that boys have more muscle and bone growth during adolescence, which requires a higher consumption of protein, iron, calcium, and zinc. For girls, adolescence means a smaller increase in muscle mass and an increase in fatty tissue because the body is preparing for menstruation. This results in a lower need for girls than boys for certain nutrients. However, girls do need more iron and calcium because of the onset of menstruation.

As people age, they need fewer servings due to a decrease in activity level and other factors. To get all the nutrients and enough energy each day, almost everyone needs to eat at least the minimum number of servings for each group every day.

Bread, Cereal, Rice and Pasta Group

A healthy diet begins with plenty of foods from the bread, cereal, rice, and pasta group (which will be referred to as the grain group since all are made from grains such as wheat, oats, corn, or rice). It is recommended that people eat between six and eleven servings per day from this group. As such, this group is at the bottom of the pyramid and forms the base, or foundation, of a healthy diet. People need more servings each day from this group

FOOD GROUP	KEY NUTRIENTS SUPPLIED
Bread, Cereals, Rice and Pasta	Complex carbohydrates, fiber
Vegetables	Vitamins A and C
Fruits	Vitamins A and C
Milk and Milk Products	Calcium
Meat and Meat Alternatives	Protein and iron

Healthy Living **7**

than from any other. The grain group of foods provides the nutrients complex carbohydrates (starch and fiber), vitamins, and minerals to the body.

The choices people make from this group are significant because carbohydrates, especially those from whole grain sources, can play an important part in healthful eating. Complex carbohydrates are the starches that come mainly from plant foods such as wheat, oats, and rice. Fruits and vegetables also provide complex carbohydrates. Complex carbohydrates provide your body with its preferred source of energy. There is a common misconception that the foods from this group are fattening. In fact, most grain group foods are low in fat and calories. Donuts, pastries, muffins and some crackers (butter or cheese flavored) can be quite high in fat and are the few exceptions. What can increase the amount of fat and calories is what people add to grain foods. For example, the butter or cream cheese people may use on a bagel can (depending on how much is used) nearly double the calories from this grain food.

Fiber is the tough or stringy part of plant foods like grains, fruits, and vegetables, therefore sometimes referred to as "roughage." People do not digest most dietary fiber, and so it gets pushed through the digestive tract helping the body rid of wastes. To get the fiber the body needs, the type of grain group foods people choose is very important. Grains high in fiber include whole wheat bread, brown rice, whole-wheat crackers, pasta, and whole grain cereals (like Cheerios, Raisin Bran, and Shredded Wheat).

Vegetable Group and Fruit Group

It is recommended that everyone eat at least five servings per day from this category. Fruits and vegetables—especially raw (or uncooked) fruits and vegetables—help reduce the risk for heart disease and some cancers by providing important vitamins and minerals as well as a good source of fiber. Fruits and vegetables are also naturally low in fat and calories, help maintain a healthy weight, and decrease the risk of diabetes and high blood pressure. Two of the vitamins that are particularly important to health that fruits and vegetables provide are Vitamins A and C.

Vitamin A is important for: night vision, healthy skin, gums and teeth. Good sources of Vitamin A are: carrots, sweet potatoes, spinach, grapefruit, cantaloupe, and nectarines. Vitamin C is important for healthy gums and teeth, healing cuts and scrapes, and strong bone development. Good sources of Vitamin C are: broccoli, tomatoes, green pepper, 100% orange juice, pineapple, and peaches.

GRAIN GROUP CHOICES

Typical grain foods include bread, cereal, popcorn, pretzels, flour tortillas, rice, noodles, and crackers. Each of the following counts as one serving from the grain group:

- 1 slice of bread
- 1/2 hamburger or hot dog bun
- 1 ounce cold cereal
- 1/2 cup of pasta, rice or hot cereal
- 3 to 4 saltine-type crackers

Most Americans don't get enough servings of fruits and vegetables every day. The National Cancer Institute and Department of Health and Human Services has been promoting increased consumption of fruits and vegetables through a program called "5 A Day for Better Health." Research has suggested that people who eat lots of fruits and vegetables may have lower risks for some cancers than people who eat less. The fiber, vitamins, and other components in fruits and vegetables may be responsible for this lower risk.

Eating a variety of fruits and vegetables every day is important since they all don't provide the same vitamins and minerals in the same amounts. Besides the vast number of different fruits and vegetables, fruit juice and vegetable juice are also considered servings from these groups. Many beverages on the market today call themselves juice but are mostly based on a sugar-sweetened liquid with only a small amount of fruit juice added. Consumers should be sure to look for the words "100% fruit or vegetable juice" on the label of juices to be sure that they contain all of the benefits of a fruit or vegetable serving.

FRUIT & VEGGIE CHOICES

Each of the following counts as a serving from the vegetable group:

- 1/2 cup cooked or chopped raw vegetable
- 1 cup lettuce or salad greens
- 3/4 cup vegetable juice
- 10 French fries

Each of the following counts as a serving from the fruit group:

- 1 medium piece of fruit or melon wedge
- 1/2 cup 100% fruit juice
- 1/2 cup chopped, cooked or canned fruit

Milk and Milk Products Group

It is recommended that two to three servings from this group be consumed per day.

The milk and milk products group includes milk, yogurt, and cheese. The key nutrient supplied by this group is the mineral calcium, but milk and milk products also provide protein, carbohydrates, and other vitamins and minerals. Vitamin D is an important component in milk because a body needs vitamin D in order to properly absorb calcium. As a result, all milk sold in stores is fortified with Vitamin D.

There are many choices when it comes to buying milk at the grocery store or even in the school cafeteria. There are four types of milk, which differ only in the amount of fat and calories they contain. All four types of milk provide the same amount of calcium and other nutrients. Water is not added to low fat or nonfat milk, although people tend to think this because the

Munching on an apple is a good way to help reach your daily fruit requirement. (Photograph by Robert J. Huffman. Field Mark Publications. Reproduced by permission.)

MILK GROUP CHOICES

Each of the following counts as a serving from the milk and milk products group:

- 1 cup milk or yogurt (preferably low-fat)
- 1 cup frozen yogurt
- 1-1/2 ounces of natural cheese (cheddar, Swiss)
- 2 ounces of processed cheese

milk may seem "watery" if they are used to drinking milk with higher fat content (milk with higher fat content tends to be thicker or creamier than nonfat milk).

According to health experts, in order to get all of the nutrition milk has to offer without getting too much fat or calories, anyone above the age of two should be drinking low-fat milk. One cup of whole milk (4% fat) has the same amount of fat as three strips of bacon. Babies and children under two years of age need that extra fat in their diets for growth and development. Most adults, teens, and schoolage children should drink low fat or nonfat milk. Low-fat (1% fat) and nonfat milk (skim milk) are excellent sources of calcium without a lot of fat and calories.

Type of Milk	Fat (per 1 cup)	Calories (per 1 cup)
Whole milk (4%)	8 grams	150 calories
Reduced fat milk (2%)	5 grams	120 calories
Low-fat milk (1%)	2.5 grams	100 calories
Nonfat milk (skim)	0	80 calories

A WORD ABOUT CALCIUM

More than 80 percent of teenagers, particularly girls, do not get enough calcium. Calcium is very important for building strong bones, improving nerve impulses and blood clotting and muscle contractions. During the teen years, people need more calcium because they're growing taller and bone development shifts into high gear. Nearly half of all bone is formed during the teenage years. Calcium is deposited in bones when people eat food rich in calcium. Calcium is withdrawn from bones when people are not receiving enough calcium; similar to the way people do their banking, calcium is deposited and withdrawn from bones on a continual basis and it is perfectly normal to withdraw from time to time. Teens and others run into problems, though, when more calcium is continually withdrawn than is deposited, meaning that teens are not getting enough of this important nutrient. When teenagers do not meet the daily requirement for calcium, their bones may not reach their full potential. What results is bone that is less dense (like Swiss cheese) and less

able to withstand the natural loss that comes with aging.

When bone loss is excessive, bones can become brittle and weak and are more likely to fracture or break. This condition is referred to as osteoporosis, or "porous bones." People are more likely to develop osteoporosis later in life if they do not reach their bone potential by getting enough calcium during the teen years. Nearly 25 million Americans have osteoporosis and four out of every five are women.

Most teenagers don't meet the requirement for calcium because of poor eating habits, meal skipping, and dieting. Two to three servings from the milk and dairy food groups each day are all that is needed to meet the daily requirement, although there is some debate over this; certain nutritionists believe that four servings of dairy a day may be more appropriate for teens. Milk drinking often declines during the teen years as soda and sweetened beverage intake goes up. Other foods in the food pyramid besides milk and dairy foods can also provide calcium, but milk is still the best source.

I can't help it. Women of all ages look up to me. Why? I'm 6 foot 2. Thanks in part to milk. The calcium helps bones grow strong. Considering 15% of your adult height is added when you're a teenager, that's good to know. Especially if you want to impress, let's say, an older woman.

got milk?

The popular "Got Milk?" campaign spreads the word about the benefits of drinking enough milk each day. (Milk Processor Education Program. Reproduced by permission.)

Experts recommend that if people find it difficult to adjust to drinking low-fat milk, they should try switching to reduced-fat milk (2%) first. Then, when they have adjusted to the change, they can make the healthy switch to low-fat or nonfat milk.

Meat and Meat Alternatives Group

The meat and meat alternatives group provides the key nutrients protein and iron. Protein is needed for maintaining muscles, and iron is needed for healthy blood. This is perhaps the most diverse food group of them all because it includes not only red meat, like steak or hamburger, but poultry, fish and seafood, eggs, beans, nuts, and peanut butter as well. These foods are considered alternatives or substitutes for meat because they are all good sources of the key nutrients protein and iron. It is recommended that two to three servings from this group be consumed each day.

In general, most Americans get enough protein each day, and usually more than they need. The foods in this group are often thought of as being high in fat and cholesterol. Some choices in this group are much higher in fat than others and should be chosen less often. Highest fat choices include bologna, salami, hot dogs, regular ground beef, fried chicken, and sausage. Lean meat, chicken and turkey without the skin, fish, and beans are the best to choose most often because they are lower in fat.

Individuals who follow a vegetarian (meatless) diet must take care to incorporate protein into their diets. People choose to be vegetarian for a variety of reasons: religion, culture, or love of animals. Whatever the reason, foods such as nuts, eggs, seeds, beans, peanut butter, tofu or possibly fish would replace meat or poultry as protein sources in their diet. If it is planned carefully to make sure important nutrients are not lacking, a vegetarian diet can be a healthy and adequate diet.

Fats, Oils, and Sweets

The small tip of the Food Guide Pyramid shows fats, oils, and sweets and is not considered a major food group. These foods provide fat, sugar, and calories but few nutrients and should be enjoyed as occasional extras, not in place of foods in the major food groups. The foods found in this group include salad dressing, butter, margarine, soda, candy, chips, and sweet desserts. Although fat is an essential nutrient needed for good health, there is no recommended number of servings provided for this group. Eating foods from the major food groups should provide all of the fat people need. The foods in this category should be used sparingly.

The Facts on Fat

Fat is an essential nutrient needed for good health. Most Americans, however, eat too much of it. Fat has been given a great deal of attention in recent years for two reasons. First, fat provides

MEAT/PROTEIN GROUP CHOICES

Each of the following counts as a serving from the meat/protein group:

- 3 ounces (about the size and thickness of a deck of cards) cooked meat or poultry or fish
- 1/2 cup cooked beans
- 1 egg
- 2 tablespoons peanut butter

more calories than any other nutrient. Second, a fatty diet can promote heart disease, cancer, and obesity (being very overweight) and is the biggest nutrition concern among Americans. Not all fats are created equal, however. There are two major types of fat: saturated fat and unsaturated fat. There is also a substance known as cholesterol, but it is not the same as fat.

SATURATED FAT. Saturated fat is also referred to as the "bad" fat because it is the type that is responsible for clogging the arteries and raising blood cholesterol levels. Saturated fats are fats that are solid at room temperature, such as margarine, butter, lard, or the fats in and on meat. In comparison, unsaturated fats are liquids. Foods that contain a lot of saturated fat are ground beef, bacon, sausage, hot dogs, bologna, whole and 2% milk, cheese, ice cream, and butter. Many baked goods and snack foods are also high in saturated fats.

UNSATURATED FAT. Unsaturated fat is also known as the "good" fat because it does not clog arteries. But that does not mean people can eat all of the unsaturated fat they want. Too much fat of any kind can be unhealthy. Unsaturated fats are fats that are liquid at room temperature like vegetable oil.

CHOLESTEROL. Cholesterol, a cousin to fat, is a steroid found only in foods that come from animals, like egg yolks, organ meats, and cheese. Foods low in cholesterol are not necessarily low in fat. An example is vegetable oil; it is 100 percent fat but has no cholesterol because it comes from a plant and not an animal.

Saturated fat and cholesterol in food can raise the body's blood cholesterol level. A high blood cholesterol level is one of the risks for heart disease. Heart disease is the clogging of the arteries, and it happens over a long period of time. It starts in the teen years and can eventually lead to a

MORE ON IRON

The mineral iron is needed to keep your blood healthy. It delivers oxygen to all of your body tissues. A low iron level in the blood is called iron-deficiency anemia and is very common during the teenage years. It is more common in girls who are menstruating than in boys, but it remains a common nutrition problem among this age group. Having anemia (low iron levels in the blood) means that blood has the reduced ability to carry oxygen to the body's cells and tissues. This can result in feeling tired, an inability to tolerate a usual amount of activity or exercise, headaches, dizziness, and feeling short of breath. It can also affect schoolwork because being tired all the time makes it more difficult to perform well in school.

To prevent anemia, include iron-rich foods at every meal. Vitamin C helps the body absorb iron from foods better and should be eaten with iron-rich foods. Not all foods from the meat and meat alternatives group are good sources of iron, however. The best sources are chicken and red meat. Beans, peanut butter, and foods from other food groups such as cereals, spinach, and raisins are also good sources of iron.

heart attack or stroke if it goes unchecked. The American Heart Association recommends a diet that provides less than 30 percent of its calories from fat. People can slow down or stop the buildup of fat and cholesterol in their arteries by making good food choices now. On the other hand, people should remember that the body still needs some fat to be healthy. Following a completely fat-free diet is harmful to a person's overall health. A fat-free diet also won't guarantee that a person won't get heart disease.

Although people do need some fat in their diets, most people get too much, especially the saturated kind. For best health, people should try to eat fewer higher fat foods. If a person follows the guidelines of the food pyramid and eats plenty of whole grains, vegetables and fruits, it isn't difficult to eat the right amount of fat. In addition, one should select milk and dairy foods made from low-fat or skim milk as well as skinless poultry, fish, and lean cuts of meat. Higher fat food choices need to be balanced with lower fat ones so that it all evens out at the end of the day.

WHAT MAKES A HEALTHY DIET?

For a healthy diet, one should:

- Eat more fruits and vegetables. Fruits and vegetables are naturally low in fat, are filling, and can help reduce cravings for higher fat snacks and treats.
- Use low-fat or nonfat milk and milk products. Milk, yogurt, cheese, and frozen desserts made from low-fat or nonfat milk will help to reduce the intake of fat.
- Eat lean meats that are baked, broiled, boiled or grilled instead of fried.

Choose these more often:	Choose these less often:
Tuna packed in water	Tuna in oil
Baked fish and steamed seafood	Fried fish and seafood
White meat chicken and turkey	Dark meat chicken and turkey
Low-fat hot dogs	Regular hot dogs
Turkey or lean ham	Bologna or salami lunchmeats
Canadian bacon or lean ham	Bacon
Turkey or low-fat sausage	Regular sausage
Lean ground beef	Regular ground beef

- Try lower fat versions of some high-fat favorites:

Try:	Instead of:
Low-fat frozen yogurt	ice cream
Low-fat salad dressing	regular salad dressing
Low-fat mayonnaise	mayonnaise
Baked tortilla chips	fried tortilla chips

Flavored rice cakes	high-fat crackers
Low-fat cream cheese	cream cheese
Low-fat fruit yogurt	regular yogurt

- Add less fat to foods. Mayonnaise, butter, cream cheese, gravy and salad dressings can add a hefty amount of fat to a meal. Try to use less of these products or find a replacement (mustard instead of mayo, jam instead of butter, etc.) or try the low-fat version to cut back on fat.

JUNK FOOD

Americans eat a lot of sugar. In fact, the average person in the United States consumes 130 pounds of sugar a year. This is the equivalent of 1/4 cup of sugar a day. Almost 25 percent of the calories the average person consumes each day comes from sugar. This far exceeds what health experts recommend—less than 10 percent.

Sugars are a form of carbohydrates. There are two types of carbohydrates, simple and complex. Simple refers to single units of sugar like table sugar. Complex carbohydrates are starches and fiber found in grain foods, fruits, and vegetables. During digestion, all carbohydrates are broken down to sugar. When most people think of sugar, they think only of white table sugar. However, sugars do occur naturally in many foods like milk, fruits, and vegetables. Less than 10 percent of the sugar that Americans consume is from natural sources. The rest is from "junk food," such as candy, soda, or processed foods.

The major nutritional concern about sugar is that it can displace other more nutritious foods in a person's diet. Sugar provides calories but no essential nutrients by itself. If people consume a lot of sugary foods, they may not have room for foods that provide vitamins, minerals, and other essential nutrients. A diet high in sugar does not cause hyperactivity as many people claim. Nor is it the cause of diabetes (a disease that disables the body from controlling the level of sugar in the blood). The only disease that sugar causes is tooth decay.

SNACKING

People often think of snacking as something bad and unhealthy. As a result, they often try to

SUGAR CONTENT OF COMMON SWEETS

To help give some perspective on the amount of sugar in each of these items, imagine dumping this many spoonfuls of sugar on to your morning bowl of cereal:

- 12-ounce can of soda — 6–11 teaspoons
- 8 ounces of Kool-Aid — 6
- Candy bar (1 ounce) — 7
- 1 cup sugar-coated cereal — 6
- 1 cup chocolate milk — 3
- 1 piece of cake with frosting — 7

GOOD SNACK CHOICES

- Cereal with low-fat milk
- Pretzels, baked tortilla chips
- Vanilla wafers
- Raw veggies dipped in salsa, hummus, or low-fat salad dressing
- Fresh fruit dipped in low-fat yogurt
- Fruit-flavored low-fat yogurt
- Light microwave popcorn
- Canned fruit, packed in its own juices
- 100% fruit juice
- Frozen yogurt or sorbet
- Pudding made with low-fat milk
- Graham crackers or animal crackers
- Low-fat granola bars
- Banana with peanut butter

prevent eating between meals. However, snacking can be an important part of a healthy diet depending on the choices people make. Many health experts recommend fueling up on several mini-meals throughout the day instead of eating three big meals. The right snacks can help boost energy levels and help people get the well-balanced variety of foods they need each day.

Snacking is not part of a healthy diet if a person fills up frequently on fatty, sugary foods. Snacks such as soda, chocolate candy, chips, cookies, cakes, doughnuts, and ice cream are not what a person should reach for first when looking for a snack. Filling up on these kinds of snacks leaves little room for the other foods people need. Even if people eat the foods they do need along with these snacks, they will probably end up with too much fat and calories in their diets. An excess of calories and fat can be harmful to a person's health. Snacks like soda, chips, chocolate and candy are okay in moderation, but snacks from one of the major food groups should be the first choice. Looking at food labels can also help a person make good snack choices. Good snack choices mean nutrient-dense snacks.

A nutrient-dense food is a food that provides a good source of nutrients in relation to its calories. For example, a cup of broccoli, a piece of custard pie, and a half-ounce of cheddar cheese all provide similar amounts of the mineral calcium. The pie by far has the most calories, the broccoli the least. The broccoli has the highest nutrient density for calcium because it provides the most calcium for the least amount of calories, which is most beneficial for the body's health. Healthy snacking means combining snacks from the different groups in the food pyramid, such as a banana with low-fat yogurt to meet a fruit and a milk serving. It's important to try to eat fewer snack foods that provide little in the way of nutrients. These snacks are usually high in calories, fat or sugar (or all three) and low in vitamins, minerals, and complex carbohydrates.

It is okay to enjoy your favorite junk food, as long as it is done in moderation. (Photograph by Robert J. Huffman. Field Mark Publications. Reproduced by permission.)

Moderation Is the Key

All foods can fit into a healthy diet. The key to healthy eating is balance, variety, and moderation. This means eating a variety of foods without getting too many calories or too much of any one nutrient, especially fat. If portion sizes are kept reasonable it's easy to eat the foods one wants and stay healthy. Favorite foods need only be reduced, not completely eliminated from the diet. Most people eat for pleasure as well as nutrition. If favorite foods are high in fat and/or sugar, the key is to moderate how much and how often they are eaten.

Not every food and every meal has to be perfect for a person to be healthy. When eating foods high in fat, salt, or sugar one should also choose foods that

Typical after-school snacks, such as chips and soda, may taste good, but do not score high in the nutrition department. (Photograph by Robert J. Huffman. Field Mark Publications. Reproduced by permission.)

aren't. If one food group is missed one day, it can be made up for the next. Food choices over several days should fit together into a healthy eating pattern.

Foods are not "good" or "bad," but a diet can be. People should not feel bad if they enjoy foods such as ice cream, candy, or chips. Favorite foods can be eaten in smaller quantities less frequently, balancing them with healthier choices to provide the variety and balance that is important in a healthy diet.

FOOD, WEIGHT, AND BODY SHAPE

Most people believe that nutrition and food are closely connected to weight and body shape. While this is true to a certain extent, it certainly does not represent the whole picture. A person's weight and body shape are not solely determined by how much a person eats or exercises. In fact, a person's body shape is determined most by the body shape of his or her parents. In addition, experts recently began questioning the role of weight and fat in relation to disease and illness. More needs to be studied, but researchers believe now that it's possible to be fit and healthy even if a person appears to be overweight. In other words, having excess fat on the body does not automatically make a person unhealthy.

A Lesson in Genetics

Nearly 55 percent of adults are considered overweight or obese in America today. It is believed that when people eat more calories than their body uses, they gain weight. Simple as it may seem, not all people who are overweight overeat. Most overweight teens do not eat more than their healthy weight peers do. The difference appears to lie in the level of activity. Genetics also can play a part. Genes are responsible for much of the way a person looks and acts. To a certain degree, they can also influence whether a person will be overweight or not. Although people may be able to improve their health by eating well and exercising, their body type and weight is dictated mostly by genetics.

Body type seems to be related to body weight. In the 1940s, scientist William H. Sheldon proposed a theory to characterize three basic body types. An endomorph is characterized by an increased proportion of body fat; a mesomorph by a muscular build; and an ectomorph by lack of much fat or muscle. An endomorph would have difficulty losing weight, have a soft body and round shape. The mesomorph would have a hard, muscular body and could gain or lose weight easily. An ectomorph would have a thin, delicate build and trouble gaining weight. Not every person will fit exactly into one category.

Having an excess of body fat can carry with it some health risk factors. Not only the amount of excess fat but the location of fat on a person's body is of importance. Women typically gain weight in their hips and buttocks giving them a pear shape. Men usually build up body fat around their bellies giving them an apple shape. Although this is not a hard and fast rule, there is evidence that people with fat in their abdomen, men or women, are more likely to develop many of the health problems associated with being overweight or obese, such as heart disease and type-II diabetes.

People whose parents are obese tend to be overweight as well. Having parents who are overweight will increase a person's chance of being overweight by 25 to 30 percent. Heredity does not destine anyone to be fat, but it can influence the amount of body fat and where fat is distributed on a person's body. To avoid serious health risks, a person who is genetically predisposed to obesity should be consistently careful about eating healthfully and exercising regularly.

The Body's Set Point

The set point theory of weight control holds that the body will defend a certain weight regardless of external factors. In other words, no matter how healthfully a person eats or how much a person may exercise, he or she remains right around the same weight. Unfortunately, many people who are overweight tend to concentrate only on losing the pounds when their focus should be to improve their health. Ultimately, fitness is more important to health than what a person weighs or the amount of body fat one has. Some individuals may not be overweight even though their weight may seem high for their height. This can be due to differences in body composition. Athletes with a lot of muscle, such as Olympic skier Picaboo Street, may weigh more than they appear, but they would never be considered overweight because muscle weighs more than fat. Ultimately, a person who exercises and eats well will naturally fall to his or her set point. Trying to fight this set point may lead to frustration, depression, and unhealthy weight management practices, such as fasting and dieting.

Body Image

Looking in the mirror—what does one see? Is it everything or is the focus just on trouble spots? Body image is how one sees oneself, and how one believes what others see, too. Body image can say a lot about one's mental and physical well-being.

A negative body image is when one doesn't like or doesn't feel satisfied with their body. Having a negative body image can be related to low self-esteem, depression, poor health habits, or a psychological disorder. It can negatively affect feelings, behaviors, interpersonal relationships, decision-making ability, and day-to-day living. It takes practice to accept one's body and understand that all aspects of appearance can't be controlled. Much of a person's appearance is due to heredity.

If a person has a negative body image, that person should strive for self-improvement but be realistic. Seeking positive supportive relationships is

Having a negative body image often leads a person to have a distorted view of his or her body weight. (Photograph by Robert J. Huffman. Field Mark Publications. Reproduced by permission.)

helpful as well as remembering that a person's sense of self-worth must come from within. Associating with people who accept themselves, recognizing that the body is only part of oneself, and focusing on positive aspects of one's personality are helpful. It's also important to practice positive self-talk often and give oneself credit for worthy accomplishments.

Food and Feelings

From the day people enter the world they have an emotional connection to food. Eating can be an emotional experience. Many people eat in response to their emotions—such as being stressed out, tired, or bored—rather than in response to internal cues that they are hungry. This is called emotional eating. People also eat in response to other external cues such as time of day, location, or social situations. People with whom we live or socialize, the places in which we carry on our lives, and our emotions largely control our eating.

"Normal" eating is defined as eating when real hunger is present and eating until one is satisfied, without feelings of guilt or becoming uncomfortably full. Normal eating is flexible and depends on internal cues to regulate it, but it also depends on good food choices to ensure good nutrition.

From birth many people are programmed to eat at certain times of the day, given food as rewards for good behavior or a job well done, or associate foods with certain holidays or social events. Many people associate eating with other behaviors such as watching television. They may find themselves frequently snacking while watching television even though they are not really hungry, because it's what they always do. And so eating "habits" are formed. Eating habits such as these can lead to overeating or eating the wrong foods. Many health experts agree that changing negative eating habits to healthier ones can help a person improve their health.

In order to begin to change a bad food habit, a person must recognize it first. The reason many overeat or eat more than they need is because they don't recognize negative food behaviors. Experts recommend that people identify their food behaviors by keeping a food diary. A food diary is a record of the food people eat, what they were doing at the time, and how they felt. This exercise will tell people about themselves, their temptations and the emotional states that encourage them to eat and otherwise ignore internal signs of hunger.

WEIGHT MANAGEMENT AND DIETING

As stated earlier, people's body weight is mostly controlled by their bodies' set point. Weight is also somewhat affected by how often

EATING DISORDERS

Eating disorders are dangerous psychological (relating to the mind) illnesses that affect millions of people, especially young women and girls. The most widely known eating disorders are anorexia nervosa and bulimia nervosa, but other eating-related disorders, such as binge-eating, exist as well. People suffering from eating disorders battle life-threatening obsessions (constant thoughts) with food and unhealthy thoughts about their body weight and shape. If untreated, these disorders can lead to serious bodily damage or even death. Recovery from an eating disorder is possible, though it is a difficult process that should be done under a doctor's supervision. The first steps toward recovery are for the sufferer to accept that there is a problem and show a willingness to focus on his or her feelings rather than on food and weight.

For more information on eating disorders, the causes and the treatments, please see Chapter 13: Eating Disorders in Volume 3 of this set.

people exercise. Many people try to change their body weight through dieting, which usually involves eating less or a combination of eating less and exercising. Some people, in an effort to lose weight quickly, may take diet pills or engage in unhealthy weight management practices. Dieting is not a healthy way to control body weight. The best way to stay healthy is to eat properly and exercise regularly. With regular exercise and good nutrition, most people will naturally fall to the weight appropriate to them, that is, their set point. In fact, experts say that when people are exercising, they need more food in order to function.

Dieting can be dangerous because it often deprives the body of the nutrients it needs to function properly. In addition, dieting can also cause people to gain weight. This happens because the body's metabolism (the rate at which the body uses energy) lowers in response to not getting enough food. Any food the body does receive is then stored as fat. This is a survival method used by the body to get the food it needs. When people go off diets, their metabolism is still lower, which means when they start eating more, they will store even more food as fat. The result is more weight gain. Experts recommend that dieting be avoided at all times. Being healthy and fit is a lifestyle choice. It doesn't happen on a temporary diet, and it doesn't happen by denying the body food. It happens when a person eats nutritious food and exercises.

FAD DIETS

Just as fads in fashion come and go, so food fads come and go. A food fad is a food or nutrition style, practice, or craze that many people adopt for a period of time. The most common food fads are related to weight loss. Usually they are the same exact diet plans that get recycled each year under a new name. Each time a promise of unbelievable weight loss is what makes the diet appealing. It may be based on special foods a person has to buy, a magical powder or drink, or a fat dissolving capsule developed to "melt away" the pounds. Fad diets usually restrict people to eating primarily one type of food and promise unbelievable weight loss in a short period of time. Fad diets are unsuccessful because they violate almost all of the principles of healthy eating.

Most food fads are short lived, but they are always replaced by a new fad. It's important to be aware of them. For example, the cabbage soup diet promises a 10- to 17-pound weight loss in just the first week of eating cabbage soup, a fat burning food. The truth is that you probably would lose weight on such a diet, but it would largely be due to loss of extra fluid (water) and because of the extreme restriction of calories. In reality, it's very difficult to eat just one food for a whole week, and it certainly isn't healthy. Sadly, with most fad diets people can spend a considerable amount of money only to be disappointed that the weight they lost (if any) reappeared as soon as they returned to their typical eating habits.

Although it may be frustrating at times when one is anxious to lose weight, it is best to lose weight slowly over a longer period of time by eating normal foods and exercising. The longer it takes to lose the weight, the more likely a person is to keep the weight off.

In addition, dieting can turn dangerous when a person engages in unhealthy behaviors, such as taking diet pills, fasting (not eating over a period of time), or purging (vomiting) the food. Many times, a diet can lead to a serious eating disorder. [*See* Chapter 13: Eating Disorders for more information.]

Weight Loss Programs and Products

Nearly 8 million Americans enroll in structured weight loss programs each year. While some programs do succeed for some individuals, unfortunately most people fail to lose the weight permanently. The problem is that most programs don't teach people how to change their eating habits and exercise regularly to promote good health. Frequently new diet books and plans appear, usually with some gimmick offering quick, painless weight loss. Many of these diets do nothing to change food behaviors permanently or create a weight maintenance program. Most are inappropriate for lifetime eating patterns, may be nutritionally inadequate, and possibly dangerous, especially for young people. For example:

Product/Program	How supposed to work	Concerns
Diet pills	Chemically decrease appetite or stimulate central nervous system	Increase blood pressure, can dehydrate, possible dependency
Special food or combinations	Grapefruit burns fat, special combinations fool your body into digesting differently and decreasing absorption of calories	Not based on scientific fact, limits choices, compromises nutrition, impossible and unhealthy to maintain
Liquid drinks or package foods	Control total calories eaten by replacing meals or snacks	Products alone do not help you lose weight, no flexibility

Any claims by weight loss programs or products that people can lose weight effortlessly are false and unhealthy. Fad diets or diet gimmicks rarely have any lasting effects since radical changes in eating habits and patterns are difficult to maintain over time. Crash diets often send a person into a cycle of quick weight loss followed by rebound weight gain.

Beware of pills and powders claiming to burn, block, or flush fat out of the body. If it sounds too good to be true, it probably is. Some diet pills may be able to control appetite but can have serious side effects. For example, amphetamines—a common appetite suppressant found in many diet pills— are highly addictive and can have damaging effects on the heart and nervous system. There are numerous weight loss programs available today. Some are schemes that come and go and others have stood the test of time. The main thing to remember is that these programs are a business like any other and aim to make money. If one plans to join a program, it pays to do some homework first. There are a few things to know before making any financial commitments to a program:

- Understand the program's format. Is it individual or group? Is it necessary to buy their food?
- Does the program offer one-on-one counseling? Does it reward or punish members based on the amount of weight lost?
- Does the program include all food groups every day? A well-balanced diet is important for good health. Beware of programs that have definitive "good" foods and "bad" foods or exclude any particular kinds of food.
- If a program utilizes its own prepackaged foods, taste them first. It would be a terrible shame to invest time and money and find the food inedible. More important, is the packaged food healthy? Check sugar and salt levels on the packages.
- Does the program fit into one's lifestyle? Is it affordable? Is it risky? Does the program help make positive behavior changes and encourage a safe personalized exercise program? These are the tools to help keep the weight off. If a program cannot provide these, then one should reconsider.
- Do the counselors in the program have an education in nutrition, psychology, and exercise?

BECOMING AN INDEPENDENT EATER

As children grow older, they often become more independent in their eating patterns. During adolescence, other factors begin to influence what people eat. For example, playing sports or engaging in after-school activities can alter eating times. Going out with friends can turn eating into a social event. Unfortunately, busy schedules and busy lives can mean unhealthy eating and poor nutrition. Sometimes, a person decides to follow a special diet, such as vegetarian or vegan. When these choices are made, it's important to make sure that the body is getting all the nutrients it needs to grow and stay healthy.

VEGETARIAN AND VEGAN DIETS

Most vegetarians don't eat meat, poultry, or fish. Their diets consist mainly of plant-based foods such as vegetables, fruits, grains, legumes (peas and beans), nuts, and seeds. Eggs and dairy products may also be excluded. Vegans (pronounced VEE-ghans) don't eat any animal products including eggs, dairy, or even honey. Others who occasionally eat meat (usually chicken or fish) may also call themselves vegetarians, although they are really only part-time vegetarians.

Only about one percent of the population in the United States is vegetarian. There are many reasons why a person may choose to be vegetarian. The most influential reason for adopting a vegetarian diet worldwide is food availability. In many parts of the world plant foods are abundant whereas animal foods are scarce or too expensive. In the United States, people have adopted a vegetarian lifestyle for one of several reasons. They may believe it is more healthful, their religious or ethical beliefs exclude meat, or they may be concerned for the environment or the treatment of animals raised for consumption. Research has shown that vegetarians have lower rates of some cancers, heart disease, high blood pressure and diabetes. Vegetarians are also less likely to have gall stones, kidney stones, and constipation.

Vegetarian foods are not just fruits and vegetables. Peanut butter, rice, tofu, pasta, among many others, help round out a vegetarian diet. (Photograph by Robert J. Huffman. Field Mark Publications. Reproduced by permission.)

Types of Vegetarian Diets

- Lacto-ovo vegetarian diet includes milk, milk products and eggs.
- Lacto-vegetarian diet includes milk and milk products.
- Vegan diet includes only plant foods.

Vegetarian diets can be healthy and adequate but may take a little more planning to ensure nutritional adequacy. This is particularly true of vegan diets. The more people restrict their diets, the more difficult it is to get all of the nutrients they need. Vegans have a difficult time getting vitamin B-12, calcium, vitamin D, and zinc because vegan diets exclude dairy and meat, both of which provide the primary sources for the aforementioned nutrients.

Becoming a vegetarian isn't as simple as some people think. It doesn't mean just excluding meat from the diet. Beginning a vegetarian diet in this manner may shortchange the body of essential nutrients important for growth and development. If one is considering a vegetarian diet for any reason, one should become educated about it and perhaps even speak with parents and doctors about a healthy eating plan. Common vegetarian foods include macaroni and cheese, spaghetti, pizza, eggplant parmesan, vegetable or bean soup, bean burritos, and peanut butter and jelly.

It's important to note, however, that growing children and pregnant or nursing women should proceed with a vegetarian diet with caution because of special nutrition needs. The key to a vegetarian diet—as with any other diet—is to eat a variety of foods and limit the amount of fats and sweets. One should be prepared with the right tools to get started and remember to eat the following foods to obtain these nutrients that could be lacking in a vegetarian diet that is not properly planned:

Protein: soy products, tofu, legumes (peas and beans), nuts, seeds. **Calcium:** milk, leafy dark green vegetables, legumes, fortified soy or rice milk, tofu. **Iron:** cereals and grains, leafy dark green vegetables. **Vitamin B-12:** dairy or eggs, supplements for vegans.

CREATING HEALTHY EATING HABITS

Eating regular meals and snacks throughout the day is very important to meeting nutritional needs. It is nearly impossible to get all nutrient needs in only one or two meals each day. This way of eating may lead to overeating and poor food choices because people may get too hungry to think clearly about what and how much they are going to eat. Irregular meals may be one of the reasons many people struggle to maintain a healthy weight. In fact, skipping meals in an effort to lose weight it is a common mistake. Depriving oneself of a meal or particular food in order to lose weight may lead to bingeing (a period of uncontrolled eating) or poor eating later in the day.

Never skip meals. Eating regular meals and snacks throughout the day is very important to meeting nutritional needs. (UPI/Corbis-Bettmann. Reproduced by permission.)

Hunger usually wins out and irrational food choices can result. Smaller, more frequent meals or snacks is a sensible way to remain energized and get all of the servings needed from the five food groups each day.

Don't Forget Breakfast

The meal most often neglected by teenagers is breakfast. It is an easy meal to skip as people rush to get out the door to school or to work, but breakfast really is the most important meal of the day. Breakfast literally means to "break a fast" (a fast is a period where little or no food is eaten), in which the fasting period is the time that the person was sleeping. A person's body needs fuel in the morning to help spark metabolism. Breakfast fuels people up with enough energy to learn and be active throughout the day. It can help to keep concentration at a better level and energy high. Breakfast can make a difference in how a person feels all day. Quick and easy breakfast ideas include granola bars, bagels, English muffins, cereal, and frozen waffles. A glass of milk and juice or fruit balances it out.

Remembering the dietary guidelines' recommendations and utilizing the food pyramid is the key to a healthy diet. Spend lots of time at the bottom of the pyramid, less time at the top, and choose carefully from the middle. Drink plenty of water each day and balance food choices with exercise to help maintain a healthy weight.

FOR MORE INFORMATION

Books

Herbert, Victor and Genell J. Subak-Sharpe, eds. *Total Nutrition: The Only Guide You'll Ever Need.* New York: St. Martin's Press, 1995.

Larson, Roberta. *The American Dietetic Association's Complete Food and Nutrition Guide.* Chicago: Chronimed Publishing, 1996.

Levchuck, Leslie. *Fuel Up!: A Girl's Guide to Eating Well.* New York: The Rosen Publishing Group, 1999.

SAMPLE EATING PLAN FOR TEENS

Breakfast

1 cup cereal (grain)

3/4 cup orange juice (fruit)

1 slice wheat toast with jam (grain/extra) or peanut butter (meat)

1 cup low-fat milk (milk)

Lunch

2–3 slices ham (meat)

2 slices wheat bread (grain)

1 teaspoon low-fat mayonnaise (extra)

Carrot and celery sticks (vegetable)

Apple (fruit)

1 cup low-fat chocolate milk (milk)

Snack

1 cup low fat fruit yogurt (milk)

3 Fig Newton cookie bars (grain)

Dinner

Grilled chicken breast (meat)

Tossed salad with low-fat salad dressing (vegetable/extra)

1 cup rice or noodles (grain)

1/2 cup spinach (vegetable)

Dinner roll with margarine (grain/extra)

1 cup low-fat milk (milk)

Snack

Light microwave popcorn (grain)

1/2 cup fruit juice or 1 serving fresh fruit (fruit)

Web sites

5 A Day for Better Health. [Online] http://www.5aday.com (Accessed October 29, 1999).

E Nutrition. [Online] http://www.enutrition.com (Accessed October 29, 1999).

Mayo Clinic Nutrition Center. [Online] http://www.mayohealth.org/mayo/common/htm/dietpage.htm (Accessed October 29, 1999).

The Vegetarian Resource Group. [Online] http://www.vrg.org (Accessed October 29, 1999).

2

Personal Care and Hygiene

Hygiene is more than just being clean. It is defined as the many practices that help people be and stay healthy. Practicing good personal hygiene is smart for two reasons. First, it helps prevent people from catching and spreading illness and disease. Second, it helps people feel good about themselves and their bodies. In American society, cleanliness is an important issue; poor hygiene is seen as unacceptable and unhealthy.

Good hygiene includes thoroughly and regularly washing one's body (especially hands), washing one's hair, brushing and flossing teeth, and caring for gums. These grooming habits will reduce the threat of bacteria that constantly reside on the body. While a certain amount of bacteria are harmless, and even beneficial, to the body, a build-up of bacteria can harm a person's health.

As children grow older, their bodies go through a number of changes. While good hygiene is important for everyone at any age, it can require greater care at the onset of puberty. When puberty arrives (usually between the ages of eight and sixteen), it means the body is becoming sexually mature. Hormones, certain chemicals made by one's body, produce both physical and emotional changes. It is the physical changes that require greater attention when it comes to hygiene. For a young girl or boy, this means taking more time and care cleaning one's body, especially the sexual organs, dealing with acne, bad breath, and a stronger body odor, as well as doing more to prevent cavities and gum disease.

This chapter will focus on all aspects of hygiene and the ways in which a person should care for the skin, hair, nails, eyes, ears, genitals, teeth, and gums.

Body Basics

Skin

Hair

Teeth

Ears

Nails

Genital Care for Females

Genital Care for Males

BODY BASICS

The best way to keep the body clean and free of infection is to wash on a daily basis. This means taking a shower or a bath and using soap and hot water to wash away the bacteria that build up over the course of the day.

This also means washing one's hands several times a day. Since the hands touch many foreign objects as well as many familiar objects (like one's nose, mouth, and eyes), washing hands, especially after going to the bathroom, will prevent harmful bacteria from damaging one's health.

Washing Hands

One of the best ways to prevent bacteria from spreading and catching the common cold is to wash one's hands. While this procedure may sound simple, medical experts say that most people don't wash their hands properly or often enough.

The U.S. Centers for Disease Control and Prevention (CDC) recommends that people wash their hands:

- before and after eating
- after touching or playing with pets and other animals
- after sneezing, coughing, or blowing one's nose
- after going to the bathroom
- after touching trash or putting out the garbage
- before and after treating a cut or wound

WORDS TO KNOW

Abscess: When pus from a tooth infection spreads to the gums.

Antibiotic: A chemical substance that can stop the spread of bacteria.

Anus: An opening in the body through which solid waste is expelled.

Bacteria: Tiny living things that have only one cell; some bacteria can cause disease.

Bladder: An organ that holds urine.

Bonding: Attaching a material to the surface of a tooth for cosmetic purposes.

Circumcision: The removal of the foreskin from the glans of the penis.

Cuticle: The skin surrounding the nail.

Electrologist: A professional trained to perform electrolysis, or the removal of hair using electric currents.

Enamel: The hard outer surface of the tooth.

Epidemic: The rapid spreading of a disease to many people at the same time.

Fluoride: A chemical compound that is added to toothpaste and drinking water to help prevent tooth decay.

Fungus: A type of plant that has no flowers or leaves and isn't green in color (a mold is a kind of fungus).

Genitalia: The reproductive organs.

Gingivitis: An inflammation of the gums that is the first stage of gum disease.

Gland: A part of the body that makes a fluid that is either used or excreted by the body; glands make sweat and bile.

Halitosis: Chronic bad breath caused by poor oral hygiene, illness, or another condition.

Hangnail: Loose skin near the base of the nail.

Hormones: Chemicals produced by the body that regulate various bodily functions.

In addition, the way people wash their hands is not always effective. For example, it's necessary to use soap and warm water, rub one's hands together vigorously, wash the front and back of the hands and the wrists, as well as under the fingernails, and then rinse. It's also recommended that the water be left running during the drying process so one can use a paper towel to turn off the faucet. In fact, a study done by Purdue University in 1997 reported that a group of children who followed a rigorous hand-washing plan greatly reduced their number of colds.

Controlling Body Odor

When a boy or girl begins to go through puberty, the body will produce more perspiration because sweat glands, some of which are located near the underarms, become more active. More perspiration means a different type of body odor, one that is stronger and similar to an adult's. Daily bathing and showering are enough to control body odor, but many people go above and beyond just washing and use different types of hygiene products that will keep the body smelling and feeling fresh.

DEODORANTS AND ANTIPERSPIRANTS. Deodorants and antiperspirants come in many varieties. Deodorants work to cover up the body odor,

Hypoallergenic: Unlikely to cause an allergic reaction.

Infection: A disease that is caused by bacteria.

Intestinal: Having to do with the intestine, the part of the body that digests food.

Keratin: A tough protein produced by the body that forms the hair and nails.

Menstruation: Monthly shedding of the lining of the uterus in females.

Parasites: Any plant or animal that lives on or in another plant or animal and gets food from it.

Periodontal disease: Gum disease, the first stage of which is gingivitis.

Pinna: Outer part of the ear; part of the ear that is visible.

Plaque: A sticky film of bacteria that grows around the teeth.

Pores: Small openings in the skin.

Protozoan: One-celled organism that can cause disease in humans.

Puberty: The onset of sexual maturation in young adults.

Sebum: An oily substance that lubricates the hair shaft.

Sterilization: A process that makes something free of living bacteria.

Toxin: A poison made by a germ.

Urethra: The tube from the bladder to outside the body through which urine is expelled.

Vaccine: A substance made up of weak bacteria and put into the body to help prevent disease.

Vagina: The female canal that leads from the cervix (or opening of the uterus) to the vulva (or the external female genitalia).

Veneer: A covering, often made of porcelain, that is placed over a tooth that is damaged or for cosmetic reasons.

while antiperspirants work to control, or dry up, perspiration. Many products now contain both a deodorant and an antiperspirant. These products come as aerosol sprays, roll-ons, sticks, creams, and even crystals. Different people prefer to use different products, and the companies that make the products will advertise specific types of deodorants and antiperspirants for men and women. This is because men and women have different body chemistries. However, these products all tend to work the same way.

PERFUMES, COLOGNES, AND SCENTED SOAPS. Many people also use some kind of perfume or cologne or a type of scented soap. While these products were first created as a way to mask or cover up body odor, many people now use them as a way to express their individuality. Not everyone likes to use these types of products, however, and some people prefer a more natural smell.

There are many different types of scents on the market, and some are advertised toward a younger audience. While there's nothing wrong with using a perfume, cologne, or a scented soap, it's important to be careful about irritating sensitive skin. Young skin can be more tender than an adult's skin, so it may be wise to wait a few years before experimenting with these products.

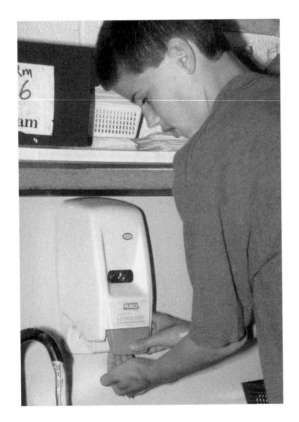

Hand-washing is a good habit to develop. (Photograph by Robert J. Huffman. Field Mark Publications. Reproduced by permission.)

SKIN

Skin is the largest organ on the body. It has two layers: the thin outer layer is made up of dead skin cells that are constantly shed and replaced by new cells. The thick inner layer is made up of blood vessels, nerves, and hair follicles, which contain glands. The glands in the hair follicles produce an oily substance called sebum, which keeps the skin and hair from drying out. Daily washing will keep the skin on the face and other areas of the body clean by removing the dirt, oil, and dead cells before they can accumulate.

Puberty and Acne

Skin changes during adolescence. The onset of puberty means more hormones are produced. It is these hormones that trigger the oil glands in the hair follicles to release more sebum, which may eventually clog the small openings in the skin, called pores.

With more sebum being produced, it's possible for the hair follicles to become clogged because the oil can't escape from the pore fast enough to make room for new sebum. If sebum and dead cells collect in the hair follicle, a white-colored plug will form in the pore. With the pore plugged, the hair follicle will begin to swell and create a whitehead. Then, if the pore remains open, the surface of the pore may darken from a chemical process that occurs in the pore, thus creating a blackhead.

OVER THE COURSE OF AN AVERAGE LIFETIME, A PERSON WILL SHED ABOUT FORTY POUNDS OF SKIN.

An actual pimple is created when the wall of the hair follicle bursts, releasing sebum and dead cells into the skin and creating a bacterial infection. Pimples are actually infections and can produce red bumps that are sometimes filled with pus. If a hair follicle bursts deep under the skin, a more serious infection, called cystic acne, will occur.

Robert Koch. (The Library of Congress)

HYGIENE THROUGH HISTORY

Though it may be hard to believe, bathing was not always considered a good practice. In fact, Saint Francis of Assisi, a Christian monk who was sainted by Pope Gregory IX in 1228, told people that they would best show their love for God by not bathing. People throughout Europe believed him and refused to bathe for any reason. In fact, Queen Isabella of Spain proudly declared that she had only bathed twice in her entire life.

It wasn't just Europeans in the Middle Ages (c. 450–1500) who refused to bathe. Early American colonists in Virginia and Pennsylvania restricted bathing as a way to outlaw any type of nudity. These laws were very strict about how often one could bathe. One law stated that anyone who bathed more than once a month would be sent to prison.

Because of these poor hygiene habits, many people died of disease. In the nineteenth century alone, millions of infant deaths were reported throughout Europe and America. The most common cause of death was infant diarrhea, which was caused by mothers who went to the bathroom, didn't wash their hands, and then passed on intestinal bacteria to their children.

It wasn't until two scientists in the late nineteenth century, Robert Koch (1843–1910) from Germany and Louis Pasteur (1822–1895) from France, discovered that bacteria were the cause of disease that the health crises began to improve. Because of their discovery, doctors and nurses began washing their hands before examining patients or performing surgery, and vaccines were developed that fought bacteria and saved the lives of millions of people.

In addition to puberty, acne can be hereditary, which means it's inherited from one's parents. Some mild skin problems can be cleared up with over-the-counter products, but more serious acne should be treated by a dermatologist (skin doctor).

TREATING ACNE. Treating mild acne generally involves using a product that helps reduce the amount of sebum and increases skin cell turnover. There are soaps, lotions, and creams that work to dry up oil and are available in the drugstore without a prescription.

Stronger treatment will usually require a prescription from a dermatologist. There are many prescription medicines, ranging from lotions to oral antibiotics that work to reduce the amount of bacteria in the skin. A dermatologist will determine the best one to treat individual problems. While acne cannot be cured, it can be treated successfully.

Basic Skin Care

Taking good care of the skin involves a few basic steps. Dermatologists recommend that a person wash the face two times a day with a mild soap or gentle cleanser. It is best to avoid washing too often, as the skin will become irritated and dry out. If too much of the skin's natural oil is washed away, the skin may become very dry and begin to itch and flake. Because the skin's natural process is interrupted, the skin may begin to produce more oil than usual, which can cause more breakouts.

Dermatologists also recommend the following for clean, healthy skin:

- Use lotions only if needed, and use ones that are oil-free and water-based.
- Try to identify what irritates the skin; if it's stress, try to reduce stress levels.
- Leave pimples alone; picking, popping, or squeezing them will only make them worse.
- Have only a dermatologist remove or extract pimples.
- Try to avoid touching the face.
- Keep hands clean by washing them often.
- Try to stay out of the sun, and use a sunscreen every day during summer and winter.

Severe acne is best treated by a dermatologist. (Photograph by Biophoto Associates. Photo Researchers, Inc. Reproduced by permission.)

Sun Protection

Protecting the skin from the damaging effects of the sun's ultraviolet rays is very important. Sunscreen not only helps prevent premature wrinkles and painful sunburns that dry out the skin, it also can help reduce the risk of developing skin cancer. It's smart to use a sunscreen with a Sun Protection Factor (SPF) of 15 or above.

Applying a sunscreen fifteen minutes before exposure will also make the product more effective. If a person is spending a lot of time outside, it's smart to reapply sunscreen every few hours, as sweat will dilute or wash away the lotion, leaving the skin unprotected. There are also some products that work while swimming, but it's always best to reapply sunscreen after swimming as well.

Sunscreen should be used every day because the sun can do damage even when it's cold or cloudy outside. If sunburn does occur, wet compresses and soothing lotions can help relieve the pain. If painful blisters or swelling appears, it's best to see a doctor.

ECZEMA

The medical term for eczema (pronounced EX-em-a) is dermatitis. The skin develops a rash in a specific area, such as the backs of the knees. It can be confined to a small area, but then spread to a larger area on the skin. Sometimes blisters appear that swell, ooze, and scab.

While eczema isn't caused by poor hygiene, the treatment for the skin disorder is dependent on regular cleaning with soap and water. Eczema can be caused by a number of things, including contact with certain cosmetics, jewelry, plants, skin cream, and chemicals used to make clothing.

Treatment for eczema includes avoiding contact with the irritating product, as well as cleaning the area on a regular basis. A doctor may also prescribe a cream or ointment to help relieve the itching that eczema causes.

Whether sunbathing or just being outdoors, it is always a smart idea to apply sunscreen to protect the skin. (UPI/Corbis-Bettmann. Reproduced by permission.)

Doctors also recommend avoiding tanning salons and sunlamps as they, too, can damage the skin.

Makeup

Using makeup is a personal choice. Experimenting with makeup can be fun. However, it's important to use products that are hypoallergenic (not allergy causing) to avoid irritation. In order to reduce the risk of clogged pores or acne, it's always smart to remove makeup at the end of the day with mild soap or another gentle cleanser.

If makeup irritates the skin, it's best to stop using it immediately. Sometimes, makeup can cause allergic reactions. Dermatologists also recommend that people avoid sharing makeup as it can increase the spread of bacteria.

HAIR

Just like skin, hair covers and protects the body. Hair is made up of tubes of keratin. Keratin is a tough protein produced by the body. Hair grows from roots in the skin, which are called follicles. Unlike the skin, which is a living organism, by the time a hair grows out of the follicle, it is already "dead." At the bottom of the follicle is the sebaceous gland. There, sebum, an oily substance that lubricates the hair shaft, is made.

Scalp Hair: The Hair on Your Head

Hair comes in a variety of types. Whether hair is curly, wavy, or straight depends upon the shape of the hair follicle. A flat follicle yields wavy hair while a round follicle produces straight hair. Very curly hair comes from oval-shaped follicles. As there are different types of hair, there are also different colors and different textures—thick or thin. Whatever kind of hair a person has, it is important that it be kept clean. This will help it look and smell good and prevent the development of scalp problems.

The hair on the head (and the scalp, for that matter) can be dry, oily, or normal, which is a combination of the two. These categories refer to the amount of sebum that accumulates on the scalp. Sebum gets distributed through the hair by combing, brushing, or touching the hair. When sebum accumulates at a normal level, it acts as a built-in conditioning system for the hair, keeping it soft and shiny.

Experimenting with makeup can be fun. (Photograph by Robert J. Huffman. Field Mark Publications. Reproduced by permission.)

The amount of sebum a person produces varies throughout his or her life. With puberty, there is a marked increase in sebum production between the ages of eleven and fifteen. From eighteen to twenty-four years of age, there isn't as much sebum being produced, and by age fifty, there is a dramatic drop-off in sebum production, which causes hair to look duller and rougher.

Most people have normal hair, which means it's neither too dry nor too oily. Those with dry hair often have chemically treated (colored, permed, or straightened) or coarse hair. While people of all ages can have oily hair, teens often have oily hair because of the increase in sebum that puberty causes.

Grooming hair often using a brush, comb, or pick is important as it helps distribute sebum through the hair. This will help hair look shinier and smoother. It will also prevent knots and tangles, both of which can lead to hair breaking or splitting.

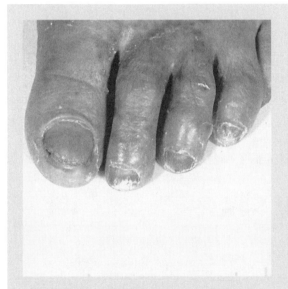

A foot infected with athlete's foot. (Custom Medical Stock Photo. Reproduced by permission.)

ATHLETE'S FOOT

One doesn't have to be an athlete to get athlete's foot. Athlete's foot, or foot ringworm, describes a type of fungus infection that occurs on the feet. It usually occurs in males over twelve years of age; it is not common with young children and women.

Athlete's foot thrives in moist, damp conditions, especially when a person is wearing tight shoes and socks in hot weather. When the feet cannot breathe due to a lack of ventilation, athlete's foot can occur. It can take different forms on different people. Sometimes, the skin between the toes will peel and crack, and at other times, blisters develop on the soles and sides of the feet. In most cases, there is an itch that accompanies these other symptoms.

When athlete's foot is diagnosed by a dermatologist (a doctor that specializes in skin), a patient will usually receive an antifungal cream to treat the problem, which generally heals in a short time. The American Academy of Dermatology recommends the following steps to prevent athlete's foot.

- Wash feet every day.

- Be sure to dry feet thoroughly, especially in between the toes.

- Only wear socks made of cotton, and change them if they get moist or damp.

- Go barefoot when at home.

- Try to wear sandals, and avoid tight shoes in warm weather.

- If possible, use an antifungal powder in tight shoes.

Shampoo and Conditioner: Keeping It Clean and Smooth

There are shampoos available for all hair types. How often a person shampoos varies and depends upon that individual's hair type. A person with dry or extremely curly hair may shampoo less often than an individual with oily or straight hair. The key to good hair hygiene is shampooing often enough to keep hair looking and smelling clean.

Conditioners can help keep hair shiny and smooth. They also offer protection against the drying effects of styling hair with heat or using styling products that contain alcohol, which can be drying too. Just as with shampooing, how often and how much conditioner a person uses will depend on hair type and styling habits. An individual with coarse, curly hair that must be straightened with a blow-dryer each day should protect hair with a good amount of conditioner; someone with limp, oily hair may opt not to use conditioner at all.

THE AVERAGE PERSON LOSES 80 SCALP HAIRS EACH DAY.

Scalp Conditions

There are some skin and scalp problems that can develop that have no relation to how clean someone's hair is. Good hair hygiene, however, can help prevent infection.

HEAD LICE. Head lice are tiny insects, or skin parasites, that burrow into the scalp. They cause itching of the scalp, which can lead to a bacterial infection because of repeated scratching. In children, however, head lice are often barely noticeable. Head lice are spread through personal contact and through sharing things such as combs, brushes, and hats. Often, the lice can make their way into a person's eyebrows, eyelashes, or facial hair. Head lice can easily turn into an epidemic (the rapid spreading of a disease to many people at the same time) at a school because children often share personal items. The problem is treatable by using a cream, lotion, or shampoo, all of which are available at pharmacies.

DANDRUFF. Dandruff, also known as seborrheic dermatitis, is a swelling of the upper layers of skin on the scalp. The first signs are a drying or a greasy scaling of the scalp. Often this is accompanied by itching. Dandruff is a condition that may be inherited, and cold weather can often make dandruff worse. Unlike head lice, dandruff is not contagious. Similarly, though, it is treatable with shampoos or solutions that are available at pharmacies.

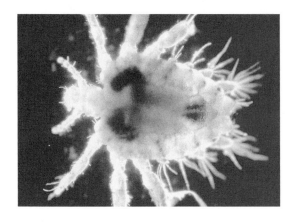

A magnification of a body louse. (Custom Medical Stock Photo. Reproduced by permission.)

Body Hair

The onset of puberty usually means an increase in the growth of body hair for both boys and girls. Hair will appear in the pubic area, and hair on the arms, underarms, legs, and face (for boys) will often grow thicker. While body hair does protect the skin and body, it is not necessary to a person's well-being. However, removing body hair is not necessary for good hygiene if a person bathes or showers on a regular basis.

Boys and Facial Hair

As facial hair continues to grow, many boys will opt to shave. How often that is done is really a personal choice, one that depends on how fast and thick the hair grows. It also depends on whether or not a beard, goatee, or mustache is desired. However often a man wishes to shave his face, a traditional or disposable razor with shaving cream or gel or an electric razor may be used for shaving facial hair.

Girls and Body Hair

Just as boys choose to shave their faces (or not), girls may opt to remove unwanted hair on their arms, face, legs, bikini (pubic) area, and underarms. There are many methods appropriate for getting rid of this hair. Remember that different methods are better suited to different body parts.

SHAVING. Using either a traditional or disposable razor and shaving cream, girls can shave their legs, underarms, and bikini area. Electric razors are also effective although many electric razors do not provide a very close shave. In fact, both methods of shaving will not remove hair at the root, which means hair will grow back more rapidly than a hair-removal method that does remove hair at the root.

TWEEZING. Plucking hairs with a pair of tweezers is a safe and clean way to remove hair; however, it only removes a single hair at a time, making it a more effective method for removing hair on the eyebrow area or removing a single, stray hair.

HAIR REMOVAL: A PERSONAL CHOICE

Choosing to remove the hair on one's body is a personal choice that is often influenced by the culture in which a person is raised. Certain cultures and religions frown upon hair removal while others enthusiastically encourage the practice. For girls, this is often a more involved decision as the American media is constantly assaulting female consumers with advertisements for products that will remove "unwanted" hair on the face, legs, underarms, and bikini area. At the height of the feminist movement in the 1970s, many women gave up shaving and waxing their leg and underarm hair. Today, many women also are opting not to remove any body hair, while others choose to do so.

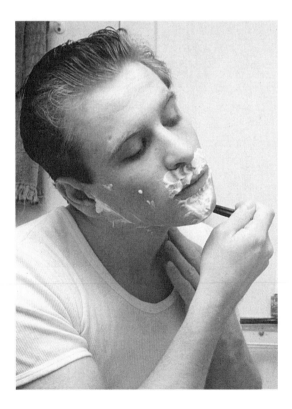

As facial hair begins to grow in, many boys will opt to shave. (Photograph (c) Margot Granitsas. Photo Researchers, Inc. Reproduced by permission.)

DEPILATORIES. Depilatories are lotions, creams, and gels that chemically dissolve body hair near the root. They tend to be time-consuming and can be messy. Also, because they contain chemicals, some people may find them irritating. Depilatories are effective for removing leg and bikini hair as well as underarm hair.

WAXING. Waxing involves warmed wax that is applied to the skin. A strip of cloth is then placed atop the wax. The strip is pulled back, removing the hair at the root. This procedure is typically done in salons and can be time-consuming. Also, waxing can often be painful and irritating to the skin. However, it pulls out the root of the hair, so waxing can last up to two months. Waxing is most effective for removing hair on the arms, bikini area, face, legs, underarms, and even the back.

SUGARING. Sugaring is a hair-removal technique, similar to waxing, in which melted sugar is applied to the skin and rolled off with the hands, removing the hair in that area in the process. Like waxing, sugaring can be used for most areas of the body and the results can last for two months. Sugaring is slightly less painful and irritating than waxing can be. Sugaring is typically offered at salons that use all-natural products.

ELECTROLYSIS. This hair-removal procedure takes place in the office of an electrologist (a professional trained to perform electrolysis). Hair is destroyed permanently at the root using an electric current. A needle is placed into the skin where the hair protrudes so that electricity can destroy the hair follicle. While the effects of electrolysis are lasting, it is a time-consuming, painful, and costly procedure (as it can take a few sessions before the hair follicle is actually destroyed). This is most appropriate for small areas of the body, such as the face.

LASER TREATMENTS. Laser treatments that remove hair are expensive and the results last only two months at first. Despite this, laser treatments are growing very popular for removing hair in the leg and bikini area. Over time, with continued treatments, results can last up to six months. However, it can take hair up to three weeks to fall out so many people shave the area after receiving treatment to prevent shedding. Also, a loss of skin pigment may be experienced in people with darker skin.

TEETH

Taking good care of one's teeth is one of the smartest investments a person can make in their health, helping to ensure that the teeth will remain strong, healthy, and white for a lifetime. While many advances have been made in dentistry and in replacing teeth, nothing can ever take the place of natural teeth. They are stronger than any artificial teeth a dental professional can make. This is why it is important to care for them properly.

Dental problems can be prevented by regularly using a toothbrush and dental floss, the tools for good teeth.

Brushing

There are many important reasons to brush the teeth every day. Brushing removes the plaque (a sticky film of bacteria that grows around the teeth) that causes tooth decay, or cavities. Brushing also helps keep gums healthy and breath fresh.

To make the most of brushing, a person should choose a soft-bristled toothbrush with a shape that suits one's mouth and allows one to reach all of the teeth easily. Use a toothpaste with fluoride (a chemical compound that is added to toothpaste and drinking water to help prevent tooth decay), hold the toothbrush at a 45-degree angle against the gums, and brush back and forth in short movements. Make certain to brush the outer, inner, and chewing surfaces (or flat surfaces) of the teeth. Brushing the tongue will help remove bacteria that can cause bad breath.

Flossing

Flossing between teeth is a very important habit to acquire. Ideally, flossing should be done every time the teeth are brushed. Using dental floss removes plaque that is caught between the teeth. This will help prevent both cavities and gum disease.

When flossing, use a generous length of floss (about 18 inches or so). Wrap one end of the floss securely around one of the middle fingers. Hook the other end around the same finger on the opposite hand. Holding the floss tightly between the thumbs and forefingers, pull the floss gently between each tooth. Softly rub the floss against the side of each tooth.

Some people have difficulty handling floss, but there are many types of interdental cleaners that accomplish the same thing as floss. These include different kinds of picks and dental sticks that can be found in a pharmacy or drug store.

Tooth Decay and Cavities

Plaque is the main cause of tooth decay, or cavities, and gum disease. When people eat, es-

BRUSH CAREFULLY!

It may sound strange, but there is such a thing as brushing teeth too vigorously. Even though brushing is vital to maintaining healthy teeth, it can be harmful if you are brushing improperly. The enamel that protects the outside of your teeth is hard but it can get worn. When enamel is worn, teeth are more prone to decay. Using gentle, short strokes when brushing helps ensure that teeth don't get damaged.

When flossing, hold the floss tightly between the thumbs and forefingers and pull the floss gently between each tooth. (Photograph by Robert J. Huffman. Field Mark Publications. Reproduced by permission.)

pecially foods containing starches and sugars, and they don't brush their teeth right away, the plaque bacteria in their mouths make acids. These acids then attack the enamel on the teeth. When this happens repeatedly, teeth will begin decaying. Cavities accompanied by painful toothaches can develop.

Gum Disease

Another problem that plaque causes is gum disease. Gum disease, which is also called periodontal disease, occurs when gums get infected. The first stage of gum disease is known as gingivitis. Gingivitis is the inflammation of the gums. Over time, the gums and the bone around the teeth can become weakened. This can cause teeth to fall out. When this happens, it means a condition known as periodontitis is present.

Unlike tooth decay, gum disease is not as obvious as tooth decay because it is painless. Some signs of gum disease include red, swollen, or sensitive gums, chronic bad breath, and gums that bleed while brushing the teeth. Even though gum disease usually affects adults, good oral hygiene as a young adult will help prevent this disease and protect the teeth.

Bad Breath

Bad breath, or halitosis, can be caused by gum disease, eating certain foods (such as garlic), or a medical disorder. Often, though, bad breath is the result of poor oral hygiene. When bacteria build up in the mouth, it can lead to a bad taste in one's mouth and a bad odor too. Regularly brushing the teeth as well as the tongue often helps eliminate bad breath.

How A Dentist Can Help

A visit to the dentist can remedy almost any dental ailments. In fact, visiting the dentist every six months can help prevent future dental ailments. Getting regular check-ups, including diagnostic X-rays, will help prevent the development of serious dental problems such as gum disease or abscesses (when pus from a tooth infection spreads to the gums). And getting teeth cleaned professionally at the dentist's office can help remove the build-up of plaque and tartar, both of which can cause cavities.

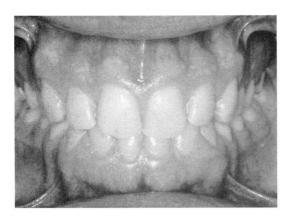

Symptoms of gingivitis include red, swollen gums. (Photograph by Edward H. Gill. Custom Medical Stock Photo. Reproduced by permission.)

Just as brushing and flossing are important weapons in the fight against tooth decay, so is seeing a dentist on a regular basis.

EARS

The ears consist of three parts: the outer ear, the middle ear, and the inner ear. In terms of hygiene, people need only be concerned with the outer ear. The outer ear consists of the pinna, the part that is visible, and the ear canal that leads toward the eardrum that separates the outer ear from the middle and inner ear.

The ear canal is self-cleaning. Wax is secreted into the ear canal by glands that are found in the skin of the canal. This wax and other particles, such as dust, travel down the ear canal and are washed away or fall out to make room for new wax being made. It is not necessary to use cotton swabs to clean the ear canal. In fact, using them can harm the ear by pushing wax toward the eardrum, where it can get stuck and cause blockage or an ear infection.

While cleaning the pinna and behind the ear is good hygiene, the rest of the ear will usually take care of itself.

PEARLY WHITES

Each year, millions of Americans go to their dentists seeking whiter, brighter smiles. Because tooth-whiteners contain peroxide, an antiseptic, whitening is safest when it is done under the direction of a dentist rather than purchasing an over-the-counter whitening kit.

Typically, teeth are whitened by a dentist using a hydrogen-peroxide solution in a custom-fitted mouthguard that the patient wears while sleeping. It can take anywhere from one to two weeks to achieve the desired shade of whiteness. How white a person's teeth get, however, depends upon the shade the teeth are when bleaching is begun. Teeth with a yellow tone will bleach whiter than those with a grayish tone.

There are other methods to lighten a person's teeth, which include laser-whitening and the use of other cosmetic procedures such as porcelain veneers or dental bonding.

Removing Excess Earwax

When earwax is pushed toward the eardrum, or when an abnormal amount of wax is produced in the ear canal, sometimes it's necessary for people to have the wax removed by a doctor. Excessive earwax can affect hearing and feel very uncomfortable. A doctor will most likely perform ear irrigation in these cases. Ear irrigation is a process in which warm water is gently flushed into the ear canal so that the earwax can dislodge and rinse away with the water.

Other times, a doctor may use different methods of earwax removal. These include using a blunt instrument that has a loop on the end. This instrument is carefully inserted into the ear canal to remove the wax. Another method involves using a vacuum that is inserted just inside the ear canal and then sucks out the excess wax.

Swimmer's Ear

The medical term for this common ear infection is external otitis. It earned its nickname because it occurs most often during the summer, when swimming is a common activity for people. Bacteria that infect the ear canal are the main cause of swimmer's ear. If there is excessive wax lingering in the ear canal, it can trap water in the ear canal. This trapped water will soften the skin in the ear canal, which makes it more vulnerable to bacteria.

When bacteria cause an infection, the ear may swell, itch, and be painful to the touch. There may also be a discharge from the ear canal, which will affect a person's hearing. The ear canal itself will be red and swollen. For treatment, a doctor will remove the infected wax and any other particles in the ear canal, and then prescribe medicine to treat the infection.

Healthy Hearing

Having healthy ears means more than just keeping them clean. It also means caring for one's hearing. According to the House Ear Institute, about 10 percent of people in the United States suffer from some type of hearing loss. The most common cause of hearing loss is loud noise. Certain types of noises, such as gunfire or firecrackers that explode near an ear, can do sudden damage to hearing. Other types of noise, such as lawn mowers and vacuum cleaners, cause damage over a longer period of time.

The institute has researched hearing loss among young people and found that there is more hearing loss among young people today than there was fifteen years ago. Loud music and the common use of earphones with portable radios and CD players probably have contributed to this hearing loss. Also, most live rock concerts have volumes that reach damaging levels. Wearing earplugs to concerts can help prevent hearing loss. Essentially, any situation in which a person must shout to be heard means it's too loud and hearing could be damaged. While many people like loud music, the smart thing to do is turn down the volume.

NAILS

Like hair, nails are formed by keratin. Tiny cells living at the base and side of the nail manufacture the keratin that produces nails. The cuticle (the skin surrounding the nail) protects these cells.

Keeping Nails Clean and Neat

Nails should always be kept clean and neatly trimmed or filed. Dirt and bacteria can get

EAR CANDLING

Ear candling is an alternative method of removing earwax that is practiced by some holistic healers. This method can be traced back to the Hopi Indians, a tribe located in North America. Ear candling is a process in which the unlit end of a beeswax candle is put over the opening of the ear canal. By covering the opening of the ear canal, a vacuum (an empty space with no air) is created between the opening and the eardrum at the end of the canal. When the candle is lit, the warmth of the candle loosens the earwax, and because the wax has no where to fall in the vacuum, it is drawn out toward the flame and collects at the bottom of the candle.

Most medical doctors do not approve of ear candling and believe it does not offer any benefits to the patient. Ear candling should not be done alone or without a skilled professional who is familiar with the procedure. It's important to check out the background and references of any healer who performs this procedure before having it done.

trapped in nails that aren't clean. As with the hands, nails are a way for bacteria to be passed from person to person. Preventing the spread of bacteria prevents the spread of illness and infection. Nails that are excessively long can, by virtue of their length, hold more dirt than shorter nails. Those with longer nails, then, need to be more diligent about keeping their nails clean. Hangnails (loose skin near the base of the nail) should be carefully trimmed with a cuticle clipper and the area kept clean to prevent infections.

Manicures and pedicures (for the toenails) can help keep nails clean and well-shaped. However, when getting a manicure or a pedicure it is helpful to have a personal kit of implements (nail file, buffer, etc.) as bacteria can easily be passed from person to person when instruments are used on different people and aren't properly sterilized (to free something from living bacteria). In fact, most nail salons now insist that customers purchase their own "kit," which the manicurist can then use on the client. Even when tending to one's

A young man shows off his multiple ear piercings. (Photograph by Robert J. Huffman. Field Mark Publications. Reproduced by permission.)

EAR PIERCING

Ear piercing is a common practice among girls, and many people consider it a rite of passage. Even boys may pierce one or both of their ears at some point in their lives. Choosing to pierce one's ears is a personal decision, however, and some people decide it's not for them. If ear piercing is done, it's very important to have it done by a professional.

Some people try to pierce their own ears. Doctors do not recommend this because, without proper sterilization, a person risks injury and infection. Ear piercing professionals use an instrument called the autoclave, which completely sterilizes equipment used in the procedure. Home methods and home ear-piercing kits do not allow a person to properly sterilize the needle used to pierce the ear. An infection can cause the ear to swell and, in more serious cases, scar the earlobe.

When ears are pierced professionally, there are aftercare instructions available that help prevent infection. These instructions usually include cleaning the lobes with alcohol or mild soap two times each day. After the ears are pierced, it usually takes a full six weeks for them to heal. Don't try to change earrings before the ears have properly healed. Patience is just as important as good hygiene. Finally, when the ears are healed, always clean new earrings with alcohol before inserting them. Also, it's not smart to share earrings without cleaning them first.

People who are allergic to certain types of metals or prone to infection should think carefully or consult with a doctor before getting their ears pierced.

CUTICLES: TO TRIM OR NOT TO TRIM

Not too long ago, if you went into a salon for a manicure or pedicure, the manicurist would push back your cuticles and cut away the excess skin. This would be done to allow for a smoother surface on which to polish the nails. Now, manicurists ask clients whether or not they wish to cut their cuticles. And there's an important reason why. The cuticle protects the integrity of the nail by "guarding" the cells that manufacture keratin, which forms the nail. If a cuticle is trimmed and becomes infected or if a cuticle is trimmed to expose a sensitive area of the nail, future growth of that nail could be compromised. Many doctors and manicurists now advise their clients not to cut their cuticles at all.

own nails, instruments should be carefully washed and sterilized with alcohol to prevent the growth of bacteria on any of the tools used in manicures or pedicures.

What Nails Can Tell a Doctor

Keeping one's nails healthy and clean is important as doctors and other healthcare professionals can often tell a lot about a patient when looking at the nails. Disorders ranging from cancer to kidney disease to malnutrition can often be detected by looking at a person's nails.

INGROWN TOENAIL. Toenails become ingrown when the edges of the nail grow into the surrounding skin. This occurs when a nail that is deformed grows improperly into the skin, or when the skin around the nail grows rapidly and covers part of the nail. Symptoms include redness and pain around the area. If the toenail becomes infected, the area will swell and blisters can develop. In mild cases, the ingrown toenail can be remedied with a simple trimming; however, many times medical attention is required. Wearing shoes that fit properly can prevent ingrown toenails. Also, it is important not to trim toenails too short.

PARONYCHIA. Paronychia, an infection around the edge of a fingernail or toenail, often begins from a break in the skin due to a hangnail, vigorous manicuring, or chronic irritation (from rubbing or picking). An infection of this type can be very painful as the nail area will swell (and because it's a small area, there isn't much room to swell). Bacteria or fungi can cause paronychia. Hot compresses can help relieve pain and may help drain any pus that has accumulated. Tending to hangnails, being careful and gentle when manicuring nails, and avoiding picking or rubbing the area around the nails may prevent paronychia.

ONYCHOMYCOSIS. This fungal infection of the nails can be contracted by walking barefoot in public places or in conjunction with the development of athlete's foot. Antifungal drugs are

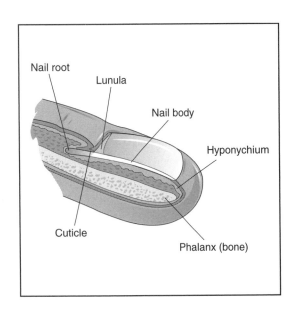

Parts of the human fingernail. (Electronic Illustrators Group. Reproduced by permission of Gale Group.)

used to treat this disorder. Keeping nails short can help minimize discomfort. Preventative measures against onychomycosis include covering the feet when walking outside the home.

NAIL RINGWORM. With nail ringworm, a fungal infection, similar to athlete's foot, infects the newest formed part of the nail. This causes the nail to grow in thick and deformed. This is treated with antifungal drugs. Keeping hands clean, particularly after being in public places such as gyms, may help prevent the transmission of nail ringworm. Also, the use of personal manicure implements can help prevent nail ringworm.

GENITAL CARE FOR FEMALES

Many females have received the false message from society that their genitals are "dirty" and that they shouldn't talk about them. Because of these messages, which can come from media as well as parents, girls are under the impression that any smell or discharge from their vagina is abnormal. It is perfectly natural to have a slight sweet smell that is nonoffensive. A strong, foul odor indicates a possible infection. With treatment, the infection will go away and so will the strong odor. Vaginal discharge is a necessary part of the body's regular functioning. Normal discharge, usually clear to white, is part of the body's self-cleaning process. As discharge leaves the body, it takes bacteria with it, which helps keep vaginal infections at bay. Discharge is also a natural lubricant, which aids in sexual intercourse.

The genitals are complex, life-giving organs with many functions. Knowledge is a key factor in developing a healthy attitude about the genitalia and realizing that the genitals are not "dirty" and are basically just other parts of the body. Understanding the normal functions of the genitals also helps a person feel more comfortable with her body and stay healthy.

Washing the Genital Area

It is important to regularly wash the genital area, including the anus, to help ward off infections and bad odor. Since the genital area is moist and warm, bacteria can grow easily. Excretions from the vagina, perspiration, and urine can build up making it even easier for the bacteria to grow. These bacteria can cause urinary tract infections (UTI's) or vaginal infections. Cleaning the genital area with a mild soap and water on a regular basis will help control the bacteria growth and limit infections.

CHARACTERISTICS OF ABNORMAL VAGINAL DISCHARGE

- bad odor
- itching or irritation
- thick, like soft cheese
- creamy or frothy
- strange color, such as green, gray, or yellow
- bloody (not during menstruation)

Vaginal Infections

Vaginal infection, or vaginitis, is most often caused by sexual contact. However, poor personal hygiene can put one at greater risk of contracting a vaginal or urinary tract infection. The following are some of the most common vaginal and urinary tract infections that can be affected by poor hygiene.

TRICHOMONIASIS. Trichomoniasis, also referred to as trich or TV, is an infection caused by a protozoan called Trichomonas vaginalis. The symptoms include a discharge that is foul-smelling, frothy, and greenish-yellow; it causes severe itching, painful and frequent urination, and, sometimes, pain in the lower abdomen.

YEAST INFECTION. A yeast infection, or candidiasis, occurs when the yeast fungus called Candida albicans, which is normally found in the vagina and anus, grows above normal levels. The result is a thick, white, cottage cheese-like discharge with itching, redness, and burning.

GARDNERELLA. Gardnerella is an another bacterium that is normally found in the vagina. An infection occurs when the amount of gardnerella bacteria increases, causing symptoms such as a gray or yellow, fishy-smelling, creamy discharge and mild itching and burning. The smell may actually become worse after washing since soap reduces acidity and bacteria grow better in a less acidic environment.

URINARY TRACT INFECTIONS. Urinary tract infections (UTI's) can occur when bacteria from the anus or vagina make their way into the urethra and bladder. Urinating helps to flush some of the bacteria from the urinary tract, but sometimes the bacteria left behind can cause an infection. Sexual intercourse, wiping from back to front, or irritants used in a bath (such as bubble bath or bath salts) are common causes of UTI's. The symptoms include painful and frequent urination, burning on urination, blood in the urine, and a fever.

What to Wash

The area that a girl should be concerned with washing is the external genital area. The internal genitals have their own self-cleaning processes. The external female genital area, or vulva, has large lips called labia majora that protect the genital area. These lips have sweat glands that produce perspiration and glands that secrete oil. If a girl has reached puberty, these lips will also have hair on them.

Beneath the labia majora are smaller lips called labia minora. In some people, the labia minora are large enough that they poke through the labia majora. This is a normal occurrence. The labia minora also contain oil and scent glands. Inside the labia minora are the openings of the urethra and vagina. Urine is expelled from the urethra. The clitoris, a small, pea-like organ that is sensitive to the touch, lies in front of the labia minora. The anus, which is not considered part of the vulva, should be washed as well. It lies in back past the lip region.

The external genitalia and the anus can be washed using a wash cloth or fingers. This can be done daily in a shower or bath or standing near a sink. Special care should be taken to open the labias and wash between them. Then rinse the area with water and towel dry.

Be Sure to Wipe Properly

Besides washing the external genital area, it is important to wipe it with toilet paper after urinating or having a bowel movement. Solid body waste expelled by the anus contains bacteria that can cause vaginal and urinary tract infections. Therefore, the proper wiping method is from the front to back. This is so the bacteria from the anal area do not make their way to the vaginal and urethral area. A person should always wash her hands after going to the bathroom.

Extra Care During Menstruation

During menstruation, the lining of the uterus is shedding and menstrual blood comes out of the vagina. While menstruation can be messy, it is easily controlled with a tampon or pad. However, once the blood is exposed to the air, it can produce an odor. A strong odor should not occur unless the person does not bathe often enough. To minimize odor and staining of clothes, washing the genital area at least once a day is recommended. It is also recommended to change a tampon every four to six hours (a pad every two to four hours), which will help control the odor and the collection of blood.

In the past, women would use cloth to collect their menstrual fluid. Some would wear cloth as an outer protection; others would bundle up the cloth and place it inside their vaginas for inner protection. Today, there are sanitary products for collecting menstrual fluid that are more absorbent, comfortable, and convenient. These products include tampons and pads. Choosing the kind of protection to use is a personal choice. Some women use only pads, some use tampons during the day and pads at night, and others use solely tampons. Pantiliners, small pads, are also available for light flows, discharge, or use with a tampon.

TAMPONS. Tampons are worn inside the vagina. Both nonvirgins and virgins can use them. Tampons cannot get lost inside the body or be pushed up into the uterus (the canal—called the cervical canal—to the uterus is too small for a tampon to fit through). They are made of absorbent cotton that is either scented or unscented and have a string attached for easy removal. (The deodorant tampons may cause irritation in some women.) Tampons are meant to be used only for menstrual flow, not vaginal discharge. They can come with or without applicators. For greater protection, some women wear

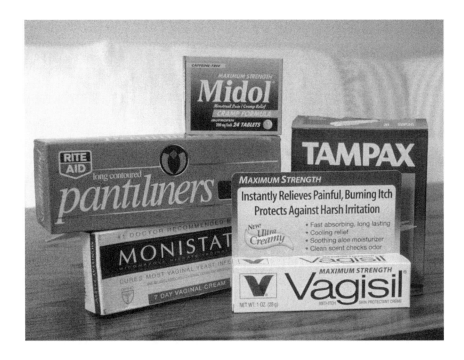

Women have a wealth of feminine hygiene products from which to choose. (Photograph by Robert J. Huffman. Field Mark Publications. Reproduced by permission.)

pantiliners when they use tampons. Tampons should be changed every four to six hours, and not worn more than eight hours. Otherwise, bacteria can build up in the vagina, which can cause toxic shock syndrome (TSS).

TSS is a rare, noncontagious disease that can be fatal. It is caused by the Staphylococcus aureus bacterium, which produces a toxin resulting in symptoms that include a sudden high fever, vomiting, diarrhea, headache, rash that looks and peels like a sunburn, achiness, and dizziness. If a person using a tampon experiences any of these symptoms, she should remove her tampon right away and contact her doctor.

Researchers have found that the risk of contracting TSS is linked to the absorbency of the tampon. The higher the absorbency the higher the risk for contracting TSS. To judge the right absorbency, a woman should monitor the amount of blood found in her tampon after she removes it. If the tampon is completely red, a person should use a tampon with a higher absorbency; if the tampon has white areas, a person should use a tampon with a lower absorbency. A way to lower the risk of contracting TSS is to switch between using a tampon and using a pad. An easy way to do this is to wear tampons during the day and pads at night.

PADS. Pads are worn outside the body. When they were first introduced, women had to use belts and pins to keep the pads in place. The belts and pins were uncomfortable, unattractive, and sometimes showed through clothes. Pads today have adhesive strips that allow a woman to attach a pad to her underwear. Today's pads are also more absorbent, allowing them to be thinner and more effective. Some even have wings that wrap around the crotch of underwear, which gives greater protection. Pads can be unscented or deodorant. The deodorant can cause irritation in some women; however, many like the deodorant products, believing they help mask odor.

DOUCHES AND FEMININE HYGIENE SPRAYS. Douches and feminine hygiene sprays are products that work to mask or limit odor or wetness. Douches are sometimes used in the treatment of certain vaginal infections. They are liquid solutions that are squeezed into the vagina. A common solution is vinegar and water. Feminine sprays are deodorant sprays for the vaginal area. Doctors have warned that these feminine products are unnecessary (unless used for medical reasons) and can cause more harm than good. This is because douches and feminine sprays can change the natural acidic balance of the vagina, which can cause bacteria to grow and put a woman at risk for infection.

Be Aware of What to Wear and Other Precautions

Another part of good hygiene is being aware of what to wear and making sure that anything that touches the vaginal area is clean. A girl should wear cotton underwear or at least ones with a cotton crotch. Underwear should be changed daily and after it becomes soiled or wet. It should also be absorbent and well ventilated. Tight or nylon underwear, tight pants, or pantyhose (most are available with cotton crotches that help increase ventilation) cause greater perspiration, which can allow bacteria to grow. Sitting around in a wet bathing suit will also contribute to bacteria growth. Towels should not be shared because they can pass along bacteria. Toilet seats are also breeding grounds for bacteria. It is wise to cover public toilet seats with toilet paper before sitting down. Taking these precautions can help lower the risk of infection and keep the genitals healthy.

GENITAL CARE FOR MALES

It is necessary for boys to pay attention to the health of their genital area. However, like girls, boys contend with societal pressures to not talk about their genitals. They are often embarrassed to speak to anyone about any problems or questions they may have about their genitals. It is important for both boys and girls to learn about their genitals, ask questions, and practice good hygiene in order to maintain health.

JOCK ITCH

Jock itch, or groin ringworm, is a fungal infection (caused by certain fungi and yeasts) that usually occurs in warm weather. It is caused by wearing tight clothes that are not well ventilated. The symptoms include redness, blisters, itchiness, and pain of the groin and upper, inner thigh area. This type of infection can easily recur if not taken care of properly. A variety of over-the-counter creams are available to remedy jock itch.

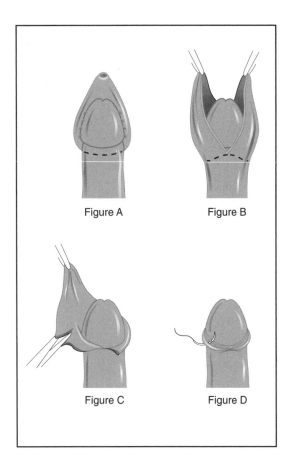

Figure A   Figure B

Figure C   Figure D

Drawing of the main steps involved in a circumcision. (Electronic Illustrators Group. Reproduced by permission of Gale Group.)

Keeping the Genital Area Clean

Boys should wash their genitals every day. This includes washing the penis, the scrotum which holds the testicles, the anus, and pubic hair (if puberty has been reached) with water and mild soap. For cleanliness after urinating, the penis should be shaken gently until the few remaining drops of urine are expelled. It may be wiped as well. Following a bowel movement, the anus should be wiped. Covering public toilet seats with toilet paper is also recommended since bacteria grows easily on toilet seats. Washing hands after urinating is a must, otherwise, bacteria will be spread via the hands.

As well as washing and wiping the genitals, boys should be concerned with the kind of underwear and pants they wear. Underwear or pants should not be too tight, and they should be well ventilated to help stem bacteria growth. If underwear gets wet or soiled, it should be changed. Also, towels should not be shared since they can pass bacteria.

Circumcised and Uncircumcised Penises

When a boy is born, he has an uncircumcised penis. This means his penis has a foreskin, or prepuce, that covers the head of the penis, or glans. The foreskin, which is about one third of the penile skin, offers protection from irritation, urine, and fecal matter. It also has sensitive nerve endings. A common procedure of removing this foreskin is called circumcision. Some people believe removal of the foreskin helps keep the penis cleaner because the foreskin can trap excretions and possibly lead to infection or disease; others believe this is an unnecessary and unhealthy procedure and that if the foreskin is washed daily, it should not pose a problem. A circumcision can be performed at any point in a man's life, but it is commonly done a few days after birth. Whether a boy is circumcised or uncircumcised, good hygiene is important.

A boy with a circumcised penis no longer has the foreskin, so he is just concerned with washing the penis with mild soap and water. If a boy is uncircumcised, the foreskin should be pulled down daily to expose the tip of the penis, which should then be washed with mild soap and water. However, do not force the foreskin down at any time. If it is painful to pull the foreskin down (and the foreskin has already detached itself from the glans), contact a physician for advice and possible treatment. Note that it is natural for the foreskin to be attached to the glans at birth and the amount of time it remains attached can vary from days to years. The average age by which the foreskin detaches is three. If the foreskin is still attached to the glans, it should never be forcibly pulled down. Just washing around the outer part of the foreskin is appropriate until the foreskin detaches. Once the foreskin does detach from the glans, it should be pulled down and the area should be washed daily.

Pulling down the foreskin and washing the area daily is important because the area under the foreskin is not well ventilated. Dead skin and an oil-like substance (called sebum, which usually doesn't appear until puberty) can accumulate under the foreskin forming a substance called smegma. This substance is a natural lubricant between the foreskin and the glans. If smegma is not washed from underneath the foreskin, it can build up and harden. This collection can lead to infections and disease. Soft smegma that is washed away on a regular basis poses no health risks; in fact, it is beneficial for erection and sexual intercourse.

FOR MORE INFORMATION

Books

Dixon, Barbara M. *Good Health for African American Kids*. New York: Crown Publishers, 1996.

Harris, Robie. *It's Perfectly Normal: Changing Bodies, Growing Up, Sex, and Sexual Health*. New York: Candlewick Press, 1996.

Jukes, Mavis. *It's a Girl Thing: How to Stay Healthy, Safe, and in Charge*. New York: Alfred A. Knopf, Inc., 1996.

Kerr, Daisy. *Keeping Clean (A Very Peculiar History)*. New York: Franklin Watts, 1995

Madaras, Lynda. *What's Happening to My Body? Book for Boys*. New York: Newmarket Press, 1988.

Madaras, Lynda. *What's Happening to My Body? Book for Girls*. New York: Newmarket Press, 1988.

McCoy, Kathy and Charles Wibblesman. *The New Teenage Body Book*. New York: Pedigree, 1992.

personal care and hygiene

Nardo, Don. *Hygiene.* New York: Chelsea House Publishers, 1993.

Powell, Jillian. *Hygiene and Your Health.* New York: Raintree/Steck Vaughn, 1997.

Siegel, Dorothy. *Dental Health.* New York: Chelsea House, 1993.

Silverstein, Alvin. *Overcoming Acne: The How and Why of Healthy Skin Care.* New York: William Morrow, 1990.

Singer, Beth Wolfensberger, ed. *The Hairy Book: The Truth About the Weirdness of Hair.* New York: Penguin USA, 1996.

3

Sexuality

Human sexuality encompasses many things. The subject has personal biological implications, social implications, and moral implications. Sexuality involves how people view themselves and behave sexually as well as how their bodies function sexually.

It is important to note that sexuality is viewed differently in different cultures. Certain practices and standards vary from country to country, religion to religion, and culture to culture. Other factors affecting the perception of sexuality, and how people react to it, include age and gender.

In this chapter, sexual development for both boys and girls will be explained, as will physical attraction and the urges and actions that accompany sexual development. Other issues related to sexuality, such as pregnancy, birth control, and sexually transmitted diseases, will also be addressed.

TALKING ABOUT SEX: IS IT TABOO?

What is the difference between sex and sexuality? The word sex can refer to gender, meaning whether an individual is male or female. It can also refer to the physical act of having sexual intercourse with another person. But sexuality encompasses much more. Sexuality includes how people learn to define themselves as sexual beings in the world. It includes desires, wishes, and dreams as well as relationships with others. It is a lot more than the physical act of sex.

Sexuality is often a difficult topic for many people to discuss, and talking openly about sexual feelings or the changes one's body is going through can make some individuals uncomfortable. Sometimes, due to a lack of open communication, young adults may receive negative or confusing messages concerning sexuality. It is important to remember that sexuality, and all of the thoughts and changes that develop as a result of growing up, are all very natural, and that everyone has questions and worries about this topic. Many teens think, "I'm the only one in the entire world with zits," or "My breasts haven't started growing yet, and I feel like an outcast," or "All the other guys in gym class seem to have bigger penises than I do," or "Why do I masturbate?" The common theme among all of these questions is, "What's wrong with me? Am I normal?" The fact is, however, that most teens are normal. They are not weird for wondering, nor are these thoughts unique to any young adult.

Sexuality is an individual experience, but the fear and frustration adolescents may feel is quite common. It's all a part of the process of growing up. Parents, teachers, and older siblings experienced many of these very same feelings, and they managed to survive the growing-up process. Armed with the proper knowledge and outlook, most teens are capable of surviving, too.

PUBERTY

Puberty is simply the time during which the secondary sexual characteristics, such as boys' voices deepening or girls' breasts growing, develop and a sign that the body's reproductive organs are becoming fully functional. Puberty occurs in boys roughly from ages thirteen to sixteen and in girls roughly

WORDS TO KNOW

Abstinence: Voluntary, self-denial of sexual intercourse.

Cervix: Narrow outer end of the uterus.

Clitoris: Small erectile organ at anterior part of the vulva.

Conception: Also called fertilization. The formation of a cell capable of developing into a new being, such as when a man's sperm fertilizes a woman's egg creating a human embryo.

Contraception: A birth control tool that prevents conception.

Cowper's glands: Two small glands on sides of the male urethra, below the prostate gland, that produce a clear, sticky fluid that is thought to coat the urethra for passage of sperm.

Cunnilingus: Oral stimulation of the vulva or clitoris.

Date rape: Also called acquaintance rape; forced sexual intercourse between a person and someone she or he is acquainted with, is friends with, or is dating.

Ejaculation: Sudden discharge of fluid (from penis).

Endometrial: Referring to mucous membrane lining the uterus.

Epididymis: System of ducts leading from the testes that holds sperm.

Estrogen: Hormone that stimulates female secondary sex characteristics.

Fallopian tubes: Pair of tubes conducting the egg from the ovary to the uterus .

Fellatio: Oral stimulation of the penis.

Hymen: Fold of mucous membrane partly closing the orifice of the vagina.

Labia majora: Outer fatty folds of the vulva (big lips).

Labia minora: Inner connective folds of the vulva (little lips).

Masturbation: Erotic stimulation of one's own genital organs.

Maturation: Process of becoming mature; developing, growing up.

between the ages of twelve and fifteen. However, this time certainly doesn't feel simple to those going through it. It is probably the first time in a person's life that he or she will have the opportunity to be truly aware of his or her own biological changes.

The experience of puberty will be new and different for both boys and girls. It is not something that happens overnight, though, but rather it is a process that occurs in stages and at different ages for different people. It is perfectly normal, for example, for one person to have already started developing while his or her best friend has not.

WHAT HAPPENS TO BOYS?

Pubescent boys can have a really hard time feeling like they fit in. That's because of the huge variation in the rate of development in boys. Two fourteen-year-old boys can look very different from one another physically. For instance, one fourteen-year-old boy can have lots of body hair, a deep voice, and be very tall, while his classmate might still be short, have no chest and other body hair, and still have a childlike voice. So why and how do boys

Menstruation: Monthly discharge of blood and tissue debris from the uterus.

Oral sex: Sexual activity involving the mouth.

Ova: Female reproductive cells; also called eggs.

Ovaries: Female reproductive organs that produce eggs and female sex hormones.

Ovulation: Discharge of mature ovum from the ovary.

Penis: Male sex organ and channel by which urine and ejaculate leave the body.

Pro-choice: Supports a woman's choice in regard to abortion.

Prostate gland: A muscular glandular body situated at the base of the male urethra.

Right-to-life: Supports anti-abortion (with possible exceptions for incest and rape) movement.

Scrotum: External pouch that contains the testes.

Sexual abuse: All levels of sexual contact against anyone's will, including inappropriate touching, kissing, and intercourse.

Sexual harassment: All unwanted and unsolicited sexual advances, talk, and behavior.

Sexual intercourse: Involves genital contact between individuals.

Smegma: Cheesy sebaceous matter that collects between the penis and the foreskin.

Sperm: Male reproductive cell.

Testicles: Male reproductive gland that produces sperm.

Testosterone: Hormone produced by testes.

Urethra: Canal that carries urine from the bladder.

Uterus: Womb; female organ that contains and nourishes an embryo/fetus.

Vagina: Canal that leads from the uterus to external opening of genital canal.

Vas deferens: Spermatic duct connected to the epididymis and seminal vesicle.

Vulva: External parts of the female genital organs.

change into men? The answer is in the hormones. Even in the womb, a male fetus contains small amounts of the "male" hormone—testosterone.

Male Anatomy

The male reproductive system has three parts: the testicles, scrotum, and penis. The testicles are where sperm cells are produced. At the start of puberty, the hypothalamus, pituitary, and pineal glands signal to the testicles to begin producing testosterone, the most important male hormone. Testosterone triggers male secondary sex characteristics, like the deepening of the voice, thicker body hair, facial hair, and enlargement of the genital organs. The testicles look like two small eggs in a sac. This small sac of skin that hangs under the penis is called the scrotum. It's perfectly natural for one testicle to hang lower than the other. In fact, in 70 percent of men, the left hangs lower than the right. This has a very good biological purpose: if the two testicles hung at the same length, they would both get a lot of friction from the legs.

FEMALES ALSO PRODUCE SMALL AMOUNTS OF THE MALE HORMONE TESTOSTERONE. IT IS SOMETIMES CALLED THE LIBIDO HORMONE, MEANING THAT IT STIMULATES SEXUAL DESIRE.

The Journey of the Sperm

The sperm cells are created in a series of chambers in the testicles. They grow and travel through the second part of the male reproductive system, which consists of the ducts for storage and transportation of sperm. The epididymis is a long, coiled canal that lies over each testicle. The next stop for the sperm is the vas deferens, a shorter extension of the epididymis. This takes the sperm from the scrotum to the abdominal cavity, passing to the back of the bladder and joining the seminal vesicles, and forming the ejaculatory duct where sperm is stored. The prostate gland lies against the bottom of the bladder and secretes the seminal fluid. Fluids from the seminal vesicles combine with this and carry the sperm out from the body. The prostate gland gets much bigger when males reach adolescence. (Taking care of the prostate gland by eating a healthy diet starting in adolescence can help prevent prostate problems that develop in many men later in life.) There are two tiny structures on either side of the urethra, called the cowper's glands, that produce a clear, sticky fluid that is thought to coat the urethra for passage of sperm. This is not seminal fluid, but it may contain sperm.

The third part of the male reproductive system is the penis. During arousal, the penis gets solid and erect and may eventually release the seminal fluid. The fluid is called ejaculate. This final stage of arousal is called orgasm or ejaculation. There is usually about one teaspoon full of ejaculate emitted. Not all sexual excitement ends in orgasm, though. Sometimes the penis may become flaccid (soft) without having ejaculated after arousal. This is perfectly normal.

THE TESTICLES PRODUCE ABOUT 200 MILLION SPERM CELLS A DAY.

Facts about the Penis

There is a lot of folklore and misinformation about the penis. There are racial stereotypes about penis size and often an unspoken competition between boys about the size of their penises. Many young men are very concerned about having a large penis. They are worried that when they start having sex, their penis will be too small to please a woman sexually or that they will be made fun of by other men. Size of the penis is not the most important factor in terms of pleasurable intercourse for a woman. There are many other aspects of sex, such as caring feelings between the sex partners, that play a more important role than penis size.

Penises come in all shapes, sizes, and shades. Some boys have birthmarks on their penises, just like people have on other parts of their body. (If there is any mark on the penis that wasn't previously noticed or some mark has changed in size, color or texture, a physician should be consulted.) Some penises, while erect, point over to the left or right, and some point up.

The penis is actually made up of spongy tissue and large blood vessels. When males become sexually excited, the blood vessels expand and more blood flows to the penis, making it erect. Although the penis is hard at this time, the skin around it stays loose to allow for expansion during erection.

ERECTIONS. Males have erections all through their lives. Even babies can have erections. Erections can also accompany the urge to urinate, and are quite common upon waking from a night's sleep. In fact, erections can seem to happen for no reason at all. However, they also occur with sexual stimulation, or when a person is sexually aroused.

NOCTURNAL EMISSIONS. Sometimes males will wake up after having ejaculated during their sleep. This is called a nocturnal emission, or the slang term "wet dream," and it is a natural occurrence. Wet dreams usually start during puberty and can happen throughout a man's life. While having a wet dream may cause a boy to feel embarrassment, it is a normal occurrence and happens to most males at some time or another.

The Stages of Development: Boys

As stated earlier, all boys have different rates of maturation. Puberty can start as early as age eight and end as late as fifteen. Boys should not be nervous if their friends start changing before they do, or if they themselves are the first to start changing. There is no rhyme or reason to development; the body develops as it is genetically programmed to do so. What, then, happens to the male body at puberty? According to *The New Teenage Body Book,* British physician Dr. J. M. Tanner identified the stages of puberty for boys as follows:

• Stage One: (approximately between ages nine and twelve)

No visible signs of development occur, but, internally, male hormones become a lot more active. Sometimes a growth spurt will begin at this time.

- Stage Two: (approximately between ages nine to fifteen)

Height will increase and the shape of the body will change. Muscle tissue and fat are developing at this time. The aureole, the dark skin around the nipple, will darken and increase in size. The testicles and scrotum will grow, but the penis probably won't. A little bit of pubic hair will begin to grow at the base of the penis.

- Stage Three: (approximately between ages eleven and sixteen)

The penis will finally start to grow during this stage. It will tend to grow in length rather than width. Pubic hair is getting darker and coarser and spreading to where the legs meet the torso. Also, boys will continue to grow in height, and even their faces will begin to appear more mature looking. The shoulders will broaden, making the hips look smaller. Muscle tissue increases and the voice will start to change and deepen. (This is because the larynx is enlarging.) Finally, facial hair will begin to develop on the upper lip.

- Stage Four: (approximately eleven to seventeen)

At this time, the penis starts to grow in width, too. The testicles and scrotum are also continuing to grow. Boys shouldn't be alarmed if hair begins to grow on the anus; this is perfectly normal. The texture of the penis is beginning to look more adult. Underarm and facial hair increases as well. Skin will get oilier, and the voice will continue to deepen.

- Stage Five: (approximately fourteen to eighteen)

Boys will be reaching their full adult height. Pubic hair and the genitals will look like an adult man's would. At this point, too, shaving may become a necessity. Some young men continue to grow past this point, even into their twenties.

Most important to remember in understanding the stages of development is that everyone has their own, individual pace. Age may vary from the approximate ages in each stage. There's no reason to worry. Inevitably, virtually everyone develops into an adult in due time.

WHAT HAPPENS TO GIRLS?

Girls usually start and finish puberty before boys. However, since their bodies are changing, too, girls have a lot of the same concerns as boys. Many girls are confused and scared of the changes they are experiencing emotionally, as well as physically. Girls often wonder if their friends and classmates are developing faster than they are. Some might be concerned because they are developing breasts faster or slower than their peers. Still others might feel uncomfortable because they are the tallest in their class. All of these feelings and changes are normal for pubescent females.

Girls usually start and finish puberty before boys. The girl pictured here is less than a year older than the boy, yet she looks much more mature. (Photograph by Robert J. Huffman. Field Mark Publications. Reproduced by permission.)

Female Anatomy

The vulva is the proper word for the entire area between a girl or woman's legs. (A common misconception is that this area is called the vagina. The vagina is actually just one part of the vulva.) There are two sets of vaginal lips. The first is the labia majora, or "big lips." This area is covered with hair in the more advanced stages of development. The outer lips protect the rest of the vagina. Underneath the labia majora are the labia minora, or "small lips" (although they aren't always small). The labia minora can vary distinctly in color, size and shape. They may be pink or brown, wrinkled or smooth. The labia minora don't have fat or padding. Instead they have blood vessels, oil glands, and scent glands. At the point where the labia minora connect lies the clitoris. The clitoris is very small but quite sensitive. It is a very important part of the experience of sexual arousal in girls and women but it may be hard to find because it is hooded with skin. Below the clitoris

THE HYMEN

The hymen, a fold of membrane at the vaginal opening, is not always visible, nor is it the main determinant of virginity (being a virgin, or one that has not had sexual intercourse). The hymen can break when girls play sports, or sometimes even with use of tampons. If the hymen is broken but one still hasn't had sexual intercourse, one is still a virgin. And some girls who have had sex may have hymens that are still intact.

Healthy Living **63**

is the urethra (the urinary opening). Below that is the vaginal opening. The hymen, a fold of membrane at the vaginal opening, may cover it.

The vaginal opening connects the inner and outer genitalia. It is possible to feel inside the long, moist canal beyond the vaginal opening. This is the actual vagina. It is even possible to feel all the way to the back of the vagina to touch the cervix. The cervix is dimple-shaped and might feel like the tip of one's nose. Beyond this dimple is the opening of the cervix, called the os. During menstruation, the flow passes through the uterus and out of the os into the vaginal canal and then out the vaginal opening.

The uterus is small and shaped like a pear. It is comprised mostly of muscle tissue, and can expand tremendously during pregnancy. Right above the uterus are the fallopian tubes. They are passages from the uterus to the ovaries, where egg cells are found. During every cycle (about a month), an egg cell is released from one of the two ovaries. This is called ovulation. During ovulation, it is possible to become pregnant if one of the eggs is fertilized by a sperm cell. This is called conception. The window for ovulation is twenty-four to seventy-two hours. This is a female's most fertile time. Sexually active women should always use protection at this time to avoid pregnancy. Women who are trying to get pregnant often chart their cycles so they know the best times to have sex. Usually during ovulation the egg that is released is unfertilized and disintegrates. The menstrual flow is made up of this tissue and the endometrial tissue that has been building up in anticipation of a new life to nourish.

The Stages of Development: Girls

Every girl matures in her own, individual way. Each person's "biological clock" is unique. Just because one person's development begins before another's has started doesn't mean that either one is abnormal. Just as it is for boys, sexual development for girls really begins in the womb. Baby girls are born with thousands of immature ova (eggs) in their ovaries. When a girl hits the age of eight, behind-the-scenes hormonal changes start to take place. Estrogen, the most important female hormone, begins to be produced by the ovaries. This starts when the brain tells the pituitary gland to begin to produce follicle-stimulating hormone (FSH). This FSH stimulates the ovaries to make estrogen. This initiates the process of puberty for females. According to *The New Teenage Body Book,* British physician Dr. J. M. Tanner identified the stages of puberty for girls as follows:

• Stage One: (approximately between the ages of eight and eleven)

The ovaries are enlarging and hormone production is starting, but external development is not yet visible.

• Stage Two: (approximately between the ages of eight and fourteen)

The first external sign of puberty is usually breast development. At first breast buds develop. The nipples will be tender and elevated. The area around the nipple (the aureole) will increase in size. The first stage of pubic hair may also be present at this time. It may be coarse and curly or fine and straight. Height and weight increase at this time. The body will get rounder and curvier.

- Stage Three: (approximately between the ages of nine and fifteen)

Breast growth continues and pubic hair gets coarser and darker. During this stage, whitish discharge from the vagina may be present, signaling that the vagina is self-cleansing. For some girls, this is the time that the first menstrual period begins.

- Stage Four: (approximately from ages ten to sixteen)

Some girls will notice that their aureoles get even darker and separate into a little mound rising above the rest of the breast. (Some girls never get this.) Pubic hair may begin to look more like the adult triangular pattern of growth. If it didn't happen in Stage Three, menarche (first menstruation) should start now. Ovulation might start now, too. But it won't necessarily occur on a regular basis. (It is possible to have regular periods even if ovulation is not occurring every month.)

- Stage Five: (approximately between ages twelve and nineteen)

This is the final stage of development. Full height should be reached by now, and young women should be ovulating regularly. Pubic hair should be filled in, and the breasts should have developed fully for the body.

Menstruation

Menstruation, or "getting your period," is the monthly shedding of blood and uterine lining that occurs when the female egg cell is not fertilized. Menstruation normally begins during the onset of puberty in females; however, as with everything else, "normal" is different for everyone. In general, a menstrual cycle is 28 to 30 days in duration (in other words, a girl can expect her period every 28 to 30 days). A period can last from 3 to 7 days. Healthy menstrual periods should at least:

- Come regularly. It's normal to skip one or two periods when first menstruating. But for girls who've been regular for a few years and suddenly start missing periods, a gynecologist should be consulted.
- Have a normal flow— not too heavy. Girls bleeding through a tampon in less than an hour are probably bleeding too much. This can make a girl overly tired from iron loss. Again, if this happens, one's doctor should be told.
- Have a normal flow—not too light. When a girl first starts to menstruate, light periods are common. But those experiencing consistently light or brief periods should not assume everything is okay. A gynecologist can help determine if this is a symptom of a more serious problem.

Healthy Living **65**

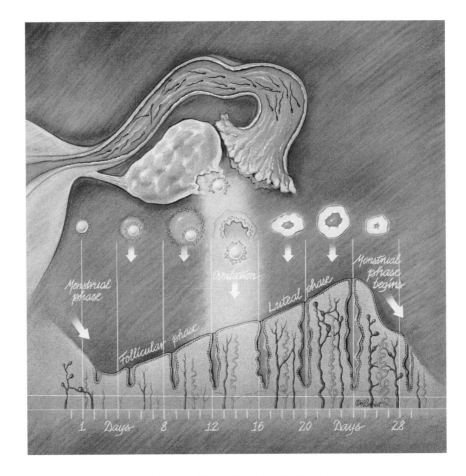

Phases of the female monthly cycle. (Illustration (c) 1996 Teri J. McDermott. Custom Medical Stock Photo. Reproduced by permission.)

Premenstrual-Syndrome (PMS)

PMS is a common complaint of young and older women alike. For years, PMS was thought of as something that women "made up" to explain their feelings—physical and emotional—around the time of their menstrual cycles. Today, PMS is accepted in the medical community as a real phenomenon that may or may not affect some women. That means girls and women can have a whole list of symptoms, or just one, or none. Some girls suffer to such an extreme that they seem to experience all the pain and symptoms of PMS. Others do not exhibit any symptoms of PMS.

PMS includes headaches or migraines; abdominal, leg, and lower-back cramps; acne; depression; anxiety; bloating; fatigue; heart palpitations; confusion; breast swelling and pain; cravings; and even proneness to accidents.

Most PMS sets in at ovulation. That means up to two weeks of every month can be filled with the above symptoms.

HEALING PMS. Girls can start to come to grips with PMS by writing all of their feelings about menstruation in a journal. They can record and reflect on all the symptoms they have, and try to figure out if the symptoms happen at the same time each month. This is the first step to healing.

The next step is addressing the symptoms themselves. One of the major causes of PMS is poor diet. What are the worst culprits? Processed foods, caffeine, sugar, dairy and meat. Sometimes simply eliminating or cutting back on these foods will cure the symptoms, but that is easier said than done. Girls seeking to beat PMS should think about eating a healthy diet based on whole foods: fruits, vegetables, soy products and whole grains.

Pharmacies also sell over-the-counter products that may help with some of the symptoms of PMS, such as reducing bloating and providing mild pain relief.

Cramps (Dysmenorrhea)

Dysmenorrhea, commonly known as cramps, may be experienced by some females during menstruation. Over-the-counter painkillers can offer a quick fix for cramps, while some women prefer to use painkillers specially formulated to also reduce bloating. (Another dietary way to prevent bloating is to reduce salt intake and drink lots of water.) Chamomile tea is a great natural muscle relaxant. However, to prevent cramps from starting in the first place, eliminating unhealthy foods from one's diet is a good thing to keep in mind. Another approach is exercise. Regular exercise will keep hormones flowing properly through the body and regulate periods, and often eliminate cramps. Doing yoga is a good way to eliminate cramps (and other symptoms of PMS as well). There are even some yoga poses that can be done which will ease the pain of cramps immediately.

If cramps and/or PMS are incapacitating, a physician should be consulted. Getting rid of cramps and PMS doesn't happen overnight. It will definitely be a process of trial and error. So if someone has PMS or even a mom, best friend, sister, or girlfriend has it, let the P stand for patience. Boys need to understand PMS too, so they are kind and compassionate to the girls and women they know who go through it.

THE NOBILITY POSE

Practicing yoga is a good way to eliminate cramps (and other symptoms of PMS as well). Yoga is a form of exercise comprised of many different poses that gently stretch and work out the muscles. One great pose for easing menstrual cramps is called the Bhadrasana or Nobility Pose. This is how to do it:

Sit on the floor and bring soles of the feet together. Close the eyes. Clasp the hands around the feet, and pull the heels as close in to the body as possible. Inhale slowly and try to keep the head, spine, and neck in a straight line. Push the knees to the floor. Hold the breath in at a comfortable level for five counts. Exhale.

Crushes

Everyone gets crushes on other people at some point in their lives. The truth is adults and even little kids can get crushes. But due to the rush of hormones that seem to "take over" young adults, crushes get really intense at the start of puberty. A crush is simply the feeling of really admiring, being attracted to, or liking someone. Both boys and girls have crushes; crushes are a fun and safe way for young people to explore their emerging sexuality, even though it doesn't always feel fun when feelings for another person are not returned. That's why they are called "crushes." The crushee can feel crushed if his or her feelings don't lead to a real romantic relationship.

There are a lot of different kinds of crushes. People get crushes on their teachers, movie stars, or people in older grades at school. People get crushes on friends of their older brothers or sisters. What do all of these kinds of crushes have in common? The objects of the crush are unattainable. That means that they are out of bounds, or aren't actual possibilities for dating because of a significant age difference or, in the case of movie stars, someone the crushee might never meet. Crushes on unattainable people are healthy

The 1984 teen movie *Sixteen Candles* depicts the awkwardness—and funny moments—of crushes and dating. (The Kobal Collection. Reproduced by permission.)

A young couple shares time together. (UPI/Corbis Bettmann. Reproduced by permission.)

and normal. As long as a crush doesn't become an obsession (thoughts that occupy the mind continually), people should enjoy their secret feelings.

Dating

Dating is when two people take a romantic interest in one another and spend time together going to movies, or to dances, or any number of places. Some kids and teens, and even some adults don't always like to use the term "dating" because it sounds too formal. Instead of dating, it may be referred to as people just kind of "hanging out" with each other. A girl might like a boy and then find out that he likes her, too. Then, she might spend time or talk on the phone with him and get to know him better. Over time, they might become boyfriend and girlfriend. If they go somewhere together, like to the movies or to dinner, they might consider that a date, but the whole process usually isn't treated as formally as it was in the past.

Kissing

Kissing is fun and, as with many things, can be perfected with practice. Lots of teens are terrified that they will end up being bad kissers, but by relaxing and doing what comes naturally most teens find that there is no such thing as a "bad" kisser. French kissing is kissing with an opened mouth and exploring one's partner's mouth with the tongue. Kissing is a great way for two people to show their feelings toward one another without going too far. In fact, some people feel kissing can often be more intimate than the act of sexual intercourse.

Petting

Petting is another term for "fooling around" or "hooking up." This is what happens when couples go beyond kissing. Petting is touching one's partner's body but not having intercourse. Clothes may be kept on during petting. However, heavy petting can advance to the stage when clothing is removed. Such petting can include oral sex and touching of the genital area and the breasts. It can arouse very strong sexual responses, including orgasm. As always, consent (permission or agreement) between the two people is really important. If one person has any reservations about progressing, something should be said. It's better to say Stop than to regret going too far.

Intimacy

Intimacy, or closeness, can be shared with someone without sharing a physical relationship. Really liking someone doesn't necessarily mean that a physical relationship is possible or even necessary. Emotional intimacy—being able to share personal feelings and thoughts—should go hand-in-hand with sharing physical intimacy. Anyone who is uncertain about taking a relationship to a physical level shouldn't do so. Often, people can share a deeper connection and more true intimacy by keeping their clothes on and finding out about a person through communication.

Homosexuality

Homosexuality, or being gay, is when a person has sexual feelings for someone of the same sex (heterosexuality is the term used for those who have sexual feelings for people of the opposite sex). It is perfectly normal to have a crush on someone of the same sex, particularly in the teen years. Many people have feelings for people of the same sex. Boy or girl, it's normal to feel deep affection for friends. For example, many females are very affectionate with one another. Does this mean that they are gay? Not necessarily. Many teenagers have anxiety about being gay. This is probably because homosexuality is often viewed negatively in American society. It's common to have sexual feelings or sexual dreams about people of the same sex. Many young people panic when this happens and wonder if they are gay. Consistent sexual feelings about people of the same sex and attraction can indicate homosexuality. These are normal feelings, too.

Bisexuality

Bisexuality is defined as attraction to and/or engaging in sexual relations with people of both sexes. Many people experiment sexually with people of both sexes. Experimenting or the temptation to do so does not necessarily make a person bisexual or homosexual. Rather, this is merely an indication of curiosity.

Some people think that those who define themselves as bisexual are just extremely open-minded and sexually free. But many bisexuals themselves often disagree. They say that they are bisexual not by choice, but because of their biology. Bisexuality is often harder to figure out, at least for young people, than homosexuality. Any teen who has such concerns should talk openly with a trusted friend, relative, or counselor to help them sort out their feelings.

SEX

Times have changed a great deal since a few decades ago. People are experimenting with sex at younger and younger ages. American culture is saturated with sexual imagery; however, sex is often presented in a taboo (forbidden) light. Often times young adults are drawn to engaging in activities that are considered taboo to them. On the other hand, abstinence, a conscious choice to abstain from sex, is gaining favor with young people. More and more teens are choosing to remain virgins until marriage. This includes boys and girls. Ideally, sex should be based on loving and tender feelings for a partner. Many people have sex based on lust rather than love. There is nothing wrong with this, if both partners consent to and enjoy the sex, but it's usually even more fulfilling if it's based on a loving union.

Intercourse

Sexual intercourse can occur when a man is sexually aroused and his penis is erect. He slides

TALK TO SOMEONE

Teens are often the worst offenders in terms of perpetuating prejudice about homosexuality, perhaps due to pressures in society to "be normal" at all costs. As a result, people who suspect they may be gay can feel desperately lonely and depressed. Many teens who attempt suicide do so because they are gay and feel they have no one to turn to.

Teens who think they might be gay or lesbian should talk to a counselor. Counselors will help a person work through his or her feelings. If it isn't possible to talk with someone at school or with another adult, the Gay and Lesbian National Hotline can be reached at 1-888-843-4564. Hotline representatives can answer all questions and make referrals to local area agencies. The Hetrick-Martin Institute in New York is a resource center for gay teens, and it can be reached at 212-674-2400.

his penis into the vagina of a consenting partner. The aroused female will produce vaginal secretions that will make it easier for the man's penis to enter her. He will move his penis in and out of her vagina in a rhythmic fashion until he ejaculates (reaches orgasm, the highest point, or climax, of sexual excitement).

Women often have orgasms during sex as well. Women usually have clitoral orgasms, but they can have vaginal orgasms, too. (For many women, it takes practice to learn to orgasm from sexual intercourse.) It is important that there is open communication between the partners so that each can share desires with the other. It's hard for both women and men to orgasm if they are tense and nervous.

Choosing to enter into a full-fledged sexual relationship that includes intercourse should never be done lightly. Both the man and woman should be mature enough and responsible enough to discuss birth control and protection from sexually transmitted diseases (see sections below) before taking that step. It is also essential to discuss one's expectations as well as how a pregnancy will be handled (see section on pregnancy) if one occurs.

Oral Sex

Oral sex is often practiced as an alternative to intercourse. Oral sex includes fellatio (pronounced fell-AY-shee-o) and cunnilingus. Fellatio is the stimulation of a man's genitals with the mouth of a partner. Cunnilingus is the stimulation of a woman's genitals with the mouth of a partner. Oral sex does not carry with it the risk of an unplanned pregnancy, as sexual intercourse does. However, it does not protect against sexually-transmitted diseases (STDs), including AIDS, because there is contact with a person's bodily fluids. When engaging in either form of oral sex, both partners should take precautions to protect themselves from STDs by using either a condom (for men) or a dental dam (a rubber shield that dentists use to isolate a specific tooth when doing work on it; used to practice safe oral sex on women).

Masturbation

Masturbation is the safest kind of sex. It is pleasuring oneself, or solo sex. It is totally natural and healthy. Most people do it, but they don't like to admit it because of the negative portrayal put upon it by society. Girls can masturbate by stimulating their clitoris or putting their fingers inside of their vaginas. Boys can masturbate by stroking or rubbing their penis. Some people believe that masturbating too often is dangerous. This is a myth. As long as something feels good, is carried out in private, and doesn't involve hurting anyone or anything, masturbation is a healthy way to explore and indulge sexual fantasies and impulses without the risk of unwanted pregnancy or STDs.

BIRTH CONTROL

Birth control has had a dual purpose in recent times, specifically where condoms are concerned. Preventing an unwanted pregnancy goes hand in hand with preventing the spread of sexually transmitted diseases, including HIV. There are many forms of birth control, or contraception, available but none offer 100 percent protection against STDs, including condoms. Ideally, both partners should be tested for HIV and STDs before engaging in a sexual relationship so that their options for birth control widen and are not limited to the condom.

Condoms

A condom is a sheath that fits snugly over the penis. The reservoir at the tip of the condom collects the semen that is ejaculated, thus preventing it from entering the vagina. Condoms are the easiest, safest, and most commonly used form of birth control. Latex condoms that are spermicidally lubricated are the most effective. Spermicidal lubricant, such as Nonoxynol-9, kills any sperm that might leak out of a condom. Some people have latex allergies; for those individuals, condoms are available in other compositions; however, they are not as effective in preventing pregnancy or the transmission of STDs as latex condoms.

Condoms are widely available, at drug and convenience stores and even supermarkets. Both sexes can purchase them; this helps both partners share responsibility for birth control. Condoms are a good way to ensure that one is always prepared (in terms of birth control) for a sexual encounter.

It is a myth that condoms lessen sexual pleasure. If one or both partners are uncomfortable using condoms, each should be tested for STDs, including HIV, and then discuss other birth-control options with a counselor or physician.

The female condom, which is similar to traditional condoms, is also available. It is placed inside a woman and it lines her vagina and blocks her cervix.

The Pill

Another common form of contraception is the birth-control pill. There are several types of birth-control pills, available by a physician's prescription only. Most common is the combination pill (which employs a combination of different

Examples of birth control products, including the Pill, condoms, sponge, and diaphragm. (Custom Medical Stock Photo. Reproduced by permission.)

hormones). This type of birth-control pill works by inhibiting the development of the egg in a woman's ovary. In other words, the ovaries remain somewhat inactive, which is similar to how a woman's body behaves when she is pregnant.

Birth-control pills are the most effective form of birth control (aside from abstinence) and are used by millions and millions of women throughout the world. However, the pill does not offer protection against sexually transmitted diseases (STDs), which leaves many women at risk for HIV and other diseases like herpes. Furthermore, the dangers of taking the pill (such as heart attack, stroke, or embolism—a sudden obstruction in a blood vessel) can be intensified by family and personal health histories and lifestyle. (It is advised that smokers over the age of thirty-five should not take the pill.) Always discuss possible side effects with a doctor. Most experts agree, however, that the possible dangers involved with an actual pregnancy and delivery outweigh the possible dangers presented by the pill. For most people, in consultation with a doctor, the pill is considered safe.

Some women have other issues with the pill, including nausea from the increased hormones, weight gain, irritability, migraines, depression, and a reduced sexual desire. These side effects usually decrease after a few monthly cycles of taking the pill. As with any prescription product, some have a great deal of difficulty with the pill while others experience no difficulty at all.

There are many pros and cons to taking birth-control pills, and these should be weighed carefully against a woman's lifestyle and health before deciding to use them.

Diaphragm

A diaphragm is a soft, round, rubber cup that fits over the cervix. It works by keeping the sperm out of the uterus. A doctor must measure a woman's cervix and prescribe the proper size diaphragm for her.

Diaphragms are used in conjunction with spermicidal jelly and are inserted thirty minutes prior to intercourse. The diaphragm must be left in place for several hours afterward. Many women enjoy diaphragms as they offer the freedom that is similar to pill usage. However, some women find diaphragms to be messy (because of the spermicide) and difficult to insert. Furthermore, the effectiveness rate is not as high as that of the pill and, unlike the condom, diaphragms offer no protection against STDs and HIV.

Cervical Cap

A cervical cap looks like a thimble with a rim. It fits over the cervix just like a thimble fits over a finger. It comes in four different sizes, and must be fitted to the user by a doctor. The cervical cap works as a diaphragm does, blocking the cervix.

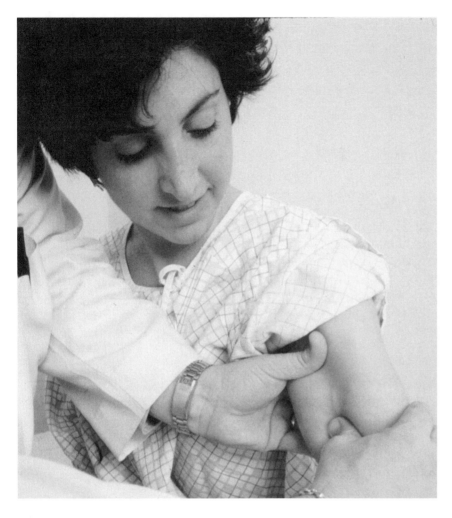

This woman has a Norplant birth control implant in her upper arm, as shown by the doctor. (Photograph (c) 1991 Linda Steinmark. Custom Medical Stock Photo. Reproduced by permission.)

Drawbacks to the cap are that it does not allow free flow of cervical fluid, which can lead to odor and infection in certain wearers. Also, like the diaphragm, the cervical cap can be difficult to insert and remove and it offers no protection against STDs, including HIV.

Intrauterine Device

Intrauterine devices (IUDs) are small devices placed in the uterus to prevent pregnancy. Though it is not known how IUDs work precisely, it is believed that they prevent fertilization. Usually comprised of plastic (copper IUDs are no longer common), most contain a synthetic hormone, often progesterone, that helps prevent pregnancy if the IUD exists in the body at a constant rate throughout a woman's entire cycle. IUDs are decreasing in popularity and are controversial as they have been known to affect fertility (the ability to become pregnant) and cause other health problems, such as rejection of the device by the body and damage to the uterus. Another drawback to IUDs is that they must be implanted and removed by a physician. Furthermore, IUDs offer no protection against STDs and HIV.

Norplant

Norplant is a contraceptive device that involves a set of thin, match-size capsules containing hormones that are implanted just under the skin of a woman's upper arm. Effective for approximately five years, Norplant has a high success rate in preventing pregnancy. Since it is implanted in the woman's arm, the woman is protected twenty-four hours a day and there is no chance of forgetting birth control (as with the pill, condoms, or the diaphragm). However, it offers no protection against HIV and other STDs; further, Norplant has many risks associated with its use, including irregular menstruation, headaches, weight gain or loss, benign (noncancerous) ovarian cysts, depression, and acne. Smokers or women with a history of certain health problems should not use it. Finally, Norplant is a very costly method of birth control (it can cost hundreds of dollars for insertion and removal is also expensive).

PREGNANCY

A planned pregnancy between two mature adults can be a beautiful experience. Ideally a pregnancy occurs between loving partners who will share the responsibility of the pregnancy. A healthy pregnancy should be free of stress. If a woman is even a little bit unsure about whether having a baby is right for her, it can affect the course of her pregnancy.

Unplanned Pregnancy

An unplanned pregnancy can be terrifying for anyone, but especially for a teenager. It can make a person feel totally out of control, especially if the parents are not emotionally connected to one another. (This is why it's so essential to practice safe sex; see box on page 81). If a girl is sexually active and using protection but misses a period, she should not assume that she isn't pregnant. There is no single form of birth control that is 100 percent effective.

For girls who are sexually active and menstruate on a relatively regular basis, if a period is late (that is, beyond the usual 28- to 30-day cycle) by even a week or two, it is best to take a pregnancy test. Pregnancy tests are administered at local clinics, such as Planned Parenthood, or at a physician's office. Home pregnancy tests are available at most pharmacies and even many supermarkets. Home pregnancy tests have drawbacks, however. First, they are not 100 percent accurate. Second, clinics and physicians provide more than just accurate results; they are qualified to discuss what options there are for dealing with a pregnancy.

A good approach to this situation is to share concerns with a trusted adult or friend, who may offer advice and comfort and ease feelings of isolation.

Choices

Going to a clinic or a physician comes with the added benefit of having all options for addressing an unexpected pregnancy explained by qualified individuals. A couple or a woman alone may choose to carry the pregnancy to term and raise the child. Adoption is also another alternative. Finally, the pregnancy may also be terminated through abortion.

ABORTION. Abortion remains a very controversial issue, and the choice to proceed with one depends on personal belief as much as the legalities of abortion in a particular state. While abortion was made legal in the United States through the *Roe v. Wade* Supreme Court case in the 1970s, many states have legislation in place requiring parental notification, something that makes abortion an undesirable or impossible choice for many minors.

Abortion is the termination of a pregnancy before the embryo or fetus is capable of surviving outside of the womb. Someone desiring to terminate her pregnancy can usually find help through a local Planned Parenthood clinic. Planned Parenthood will be familiar with area clinics and physicians that offer abortion services. The organization is also familiar with any restrictions that exist in a particular state concerning abortion.

Most abortions are performed in the first trimester (first three months) and early second trimester of the pregnancy. Having a procedure in a clinic or a hospital is an ambulatory procedure (meaning that patients are sent home the

THE RIGHT TO CHOOSE

Prior to 1973 abortion was illegal in the United States. On January 22, 1973, the US Supreme Court declared that "the right of privacy...founded in the fourteenth amendment's concept of personal liberty ...is broad enough to encompass a woman's decision whether or not to terminate her pregnancy." The court held that a woman and her doctor had the right to make a private decision about first trimester abortions. Prior to that decision, women who wanted to terminate a pregnancy had few choices. Many put their lives in danger by having "back-alley" abortions (abortions performed by laypersons that often involved unsanitary conditions and the abortionists' inability to deal with emergency situations, such as hemorrhaging). Sadly, many women lost their lives in this manner. In response to these medical mishaps and the *Roe v. Wade* ruling, the Pro-Choice movement has been working for women's rights ever since. Conversely, the Right-to-Life movement believes abortion is morally wrong as a fetus is a human being with inherent rights.

very same day). After undergoing an abortion, most women are issued antibiotics to prevent infection and given birth-control counseling. Follow-up visits to a physician are required and recipients must also abstain from sexual intercourse and wearing tampons for several weeks. Discomfort, cramps, and bleeding are common in the days following an abortion, as is emotional pain.

Some women may not be emotionally affected at all by an abortion, while others may address feelings of regret or sadness years later. Choosing abortion is not simple or easy; in fact, it can be terrifying and traumatic. However, for many women, young and older, it is still the best choice for them personally.

ADOPTION. Some young women who find themselves pregnant are opposed to abortion for moral or religious reasons. Yet for any number of reasons,

Scene from a pro-choice rally held in 1992. (Photograph (c) 1992 Kevin Beebe. Custom Medical Stock Photo. Reproduced by permission.)

they feel they are not able to raise a child on their own. For such people, carrying a child to term (until it is born) but placing the baby for adoption after the birth is a viable solution.

Adoption can be a very complicated legal process, but put very simply, when a woman or couple decide to place their baby up for adoption, they legally give up parental rights to the child so that another person or couple can legally become the child's parents. The biological parents, or birth parents, are the people who conceived and gave birth to the child. The adoptive parents have legal custody of the child and are the people who care for and raise the child as their own.

Giving up a child for adoption is never easy. Many women that have experienced pregnancy bond with the baby inside them on a very deep level. It's not easy to let go after nine months of closeness. Often, a birth mother or birth father will wonder about that child for the rest of their lives. Stories, positive and negative, about birth parents reconnecting with children they've given up for adoption years earlier are prevalent in the media. People considering adoption must make careful choices and be certain that they are willing to face the likelihood that they will never see their birth child again. People need to be honest with themselves when considering adoption and all parties should consult with attorneys experienced in such matters. However, for many people, adoption is the best choice for them personally.

SEXUALLY TRANSMITTED DISEASES

Sexually transmitted diseases (STDs) include an array of diseases, some treatable and some not, that are transmitted primarily through sexual activity. The best way to almost completely reduce the risk of catching a STD is to abstain from sexual activity. Another method to reduce the odds of becoming infected is getting tested, along with one's planned sexual partner, for STDs, including and especially for HIV.

HIV/AIDS

Human Immunodeficiency Virus (HIV) infection is an immune system disorder (the immune system helps the body resist infection by diseases) that can be contracted through sexual activity as well as other types of contact. HIV is often labelled as an STD because of the high number of cases that emerge as a result of sexual activity, but it is important to note that HIV is not always contracted through sexual activity.

HIV can lead to the development of full-blown Acquired Immunodeficiency Syndrome (AIDS), which is also an immune system disorder. People catch HIV through sexual contact or by exposure to contaminated blood (such as through sharing dirty needles or a blood transfusion). People cannot contract HIV from sharing a meal, swimming in a pool, hugging, casual kissing, holding hands, or even sharing a toothbrush. Furthermore, there are no documented cases of transmission of HIV through French kissing. HIV can remain in the systems of the body for many years without leading to the development of AIDS; however, HIV can easily be detected with a blood test.

Many myths about AIDS have circulated since it was first discovered in the early 1980s. The first, and most fatal myth to women and heterosexual men, is that AIDS is only a "gay person's disease" or a syndrome limited to intravenous drug abusers who share needles with other users. The disease did devastate the gay community in the 1980s, but gay communities around the United States quickly took up a campaign of awareness and activism that led to a sharp decline in HIV-infection rates in that population. (These numbers, however, are going up again and are a big concern in the gay and lesbian community.) The strongest growing populations currently being infected with HIV include heterosexual women and teens. Specifically, young black heterosexual females are the fastest growing group of new cases.

Anyone who has sex is at risk for catching and/or spreading HIV. This is why practicing safe sex is imperative to everyone's health.

Chlamydia

Chlamydia is the most common sexually transmitted disease. It is caused by a virus and is spread during sexual intercourse with an infected person. Girls often have no symptoms. Males are more likely to have symptoms, including irritation or burning during urination and a milky discharge from the penis in the morning. For females, the only indication of being infected with chlamydia may be vague, lower abdominal pain. As a result, women's reproductive organs may be damaged by Pelvic Inflammatory Disease if chlamydia is not treated in a timely way. Therefore, it is really important to get tested if one has had unprotected sex. The virus can be treated with antibiotics.

Gonorrhea

Gonorrhea is a STD caused by bacteria. It can occur in the cervix, penis, throat and rectum. Symptoms usually appear only in the male, similar to chlamydia. Two to nine days after infection, males will experience painful urination and a thick, yellow discharge from the penis. Boys experiencing these symptoms must inform any and all sexual partners so that those individuals can get tested and receive treatment. Gonorrhea can render women sterile (unable to have children) without treatment. It is treated with high-dose antibiotics.

Herpes

Herpes is another very common STD. Genital herpes affects 10 to 40 million Americans. The Herpes Simplex 2 virus causes it; this is the same virus that causes cold sores in and around the mouth. The herpes virus can be spread from the mouth to the genitals during oral sex. Two to twenty days after exposure, symptoms appear. Small, painful, pus-filled blisters appear on the labia, around the vagina, on the penis, and around the anus in both sexes. Swollen lymph glands, aching muscles and fever are some other symptoms. The symptoms subside after a few weeks, but the virus stays dormant in the body and can flare up regularly. It can also never flare up again. Even if there aren't any symptoms present, a person can still transmit the disease to another.

Compromised immunity and emotional stress can trigger symptoms. Sexually active individuals should be tested for herpes and all STDs even if no symptoms are present. At this time, there is no cure for genital or oral herpes. Treatment includes acyclovir, which can reduce symptoms and is available in topical and oral forms. A healthy diet and avoiding stress also are important.

Syphilis

Syphilis is a STD caused by a very small, corkscrew-shaped spirochete (bacterium). It is spread by sexual contact and can be transmitted from a sex organ to an open cut on the skin of another person. Ten to ninety days after infection, a small, painless sore can appear on the genitals. After it goes away, weeks or months later a rash can appear all over the body, and swollen glands accompanied by flu-like symptoms may occur. Untreated syphilis does

---

SAFE SEX

There are three ways to practice 100 percent safe sex. They are abstinence, waiting until marriage to have sex (as long as one's marriage partner has done the same), and solo masturbation. If you choose to be sexually active, however, there are guidelines to safer sex. The first is to be informed. Know your body and know the risks. Know your sex partner and keep lines of communication wide open. Know their history, who they have had sex with, and if they have ever been diagnosed with a STD. People in monogamous (having only one partner at a time) relationships are at a lower risk for STDs.

Very safe sex includes: kissing with closed lips, rubbing against each other with clothes on (grinding), and sharing fantasies with a partner verbally.

The guidelines for reasonably safe sex are as follows: sexual intercourse using a condom and spermicidal jelly, French kissing, oral sex with a latex barrier like the "dental dam," and mutual masturbation. Unsafe sex includes the following: sexual intercourse without a condom, oral sex without a barrier, and mutual masturbation using sex toys that are shared.

The most important thing to remember about safe sex is that it is protecting one's very life if it is practiced. It is essential to insist that a potential partner agree to safe sex; this expresses the value one places on health and well-being and one's own high level of self-esteem. No one should be afraid to talk about it. If potential partners don't want to practice or even talk about safe sex, they are bad news. That means they don't value their own life, so it's highly doubtful they value anyone else's. There are many ways to give and receive pleasure without putting one's life in danger.

not go away. The disease can remain dormant for years and reappear when it is too late. The third stage of the disease may include nervous, brain, and circulatory system damage, and possibly death. Once detected, syphilis can be treated with penicillin.

Genital Warts, or Human Papilloma Virus

Genital warts (also known as Human Papilloma Virus) is the third most common STD. The warts are extremely contagious, and can appear on the vagina, cervix, penis, and rectum or in the urethra in the male. They are white-colored and cauliflower-shaped growths. They appear a few months after exposure. A physician can remove them with podophyllin, a medication, or by nitrogen freezing or laser treatment.

Crabs, or Pubic Lice

Crabs or pubic lice are spread by sexual contact with an infected partner or even by sharing of bedding, clothing, towels and toilet seats. Crabs cause intense itching and sometimes pain where the parasites have burrowed under the skin. A prescription drug called Kwell is the most effective treatment. Over-the-counter medications are also available. Washing bedding and clothing in hot water is essential follow-up for someone infected with crabs.

A rape counselor talks with a young rape victim at the hospital. (Custom Medical Stock Photo. Reproduced by permission.)

SEXUAL HARASSMENT AND ABUSE

Sexual harassment and abuse have always been in existence, but have gotten a lot of exposure especially over the past few years. Sexual harassment includes almost all unwanted and unsolicited sexual advances, talk, and behavior. Sexual abuse includes all levels of sexual contact against anyone's will. Sexual abuse may include, but is not limited to, inappropriate touching or kissing, incest (sexual relations between closely related people), rape, and date rape. A perpetrator's motives for victimizing another are usually based around issues of power; the power is derived by having another person at his or her mercy, sexually or verbally. Sexual abuse and harassment can happen anywhere and at almost anyone's hands, from peers to a trusted adult to a total stranger.

Many people that are being harassed or abused are sometimes afraid to admit it. There are a lot of reasons for this. Sometimes the person harassing another threatens the victim, forcing him or her to promise not to tell anyone else, or threatens to harm the victim's family or that the victim might lose a job or favor with the perpetrator. Sometimes people are afraid that they are responsible for what has happened to them, so they want to keep it a secret. Young people are often manipulated into thinking that they will get into trouble if they tell an adult about the situation.

ROHYPNOL: THE "DATE RAPE DRUG"

Date rape, or acquaintance rape, is forced sexual intercourse between a person and someone she or he is acquainted with, is friends with, or is dating. That is, it occurs with someone the person knows, not a complete stranger. Often times, date rapes go unreported because it is hard for people to think that someone they know—or are even dating—would intentionally hurt them, even if they have not given consent to have sex. Rape, whether committed by an acquaintance or stranger, is a crime and should be reported to the police regardless of how well the two parties know one another.

Sometimes a date rape might occur but the victim has no memory of it. She may know that something has happened to her, or feel violated in some way, but not have a clear memory of the events. In these instances, Rohypnol, the so-called "date rape drug," may have been given to the person without her knowledge.

Rohypnol (pronounced row-hip-nole) is a powerful tranquilizer that is illegal in United States. (Outside of the United States, Rohypnol is prescribed for the treatment of sleep disorders.) The drug produces sedative (calming, tranquilizing) effects such as amnesia (loss of memory) and muscle relaxation, and the effects can last up to eight hours. Rohypnol, nicknamed "roofies" or "ruffies," has gotten the reputation as a date rape drug in recent years because of its reported use among victims of date rape who were rendered helpless—and thus not able to consent to sexual relations—under its effects.

Not all uses of Rohypnol are without the user's consent, however. According to the Teen Challenge World Wide Network, "Rohypnol use appears to be spreading in the United States among high school and college youth" to enhance the feeling of drunkenness when mixed with beer or alcohol. Whether taken intentionally, or having it "slipped" to someone without his or her knowledge, Rohypnol is a dangerous, illegal drug that renders one out of control of one's own body.

Healthy Living **83**

If anyone, an adult or another teen or child, touches anyone else inappropriately or threatens another person sexually, one should immediately tell a trusted adult or law-enforcement professional. Sometimes, the abuser or perpetrator is someone that, in normal situations, should be trusted. In this case, it is often hard to speak up, especially if that person is a classmate, a boss, or even a family member. If a victim is scared that he or she won't be believed, a neutral party should be consulted (a guidance counselor, a neighbor, a friend's mother or father) so that they can act on the victim's behalf.

The only way to stop abuse and harassment is to expose it.

FOR MORE INFORMATION

Books

Ditson, Mary, Caesar Pacifici and Lee White. *The Teenage Human Body Operator's Manual.* Ore.: Northwest Media Inc., 1998.

Harris, Robie H. *It's Perfectly Normal: Changing Bodies, Growing Up, Sex & Sexual Health.* New York: Candlewick Press, 1996.

Jukes, Mavis. *It's A Girl Thing: How To Stay Healthy, Safe and In Charge.* New York: Alfred A. Knopf, 1996.

McCoy, Kathy and Charles Wibbelsman. *The New Teenage Body Book.* New York: The Body Press/Perigee Books, 1992.

Web sites

The American Foundation for AIDS Research. [Online] http://amfar.org (Accessed October 25, 1999)

Centers for Disease Control and Prevention. [Online] http://www.cdc.gov (Accessed October 25, 1999)

Planned Parenthood. [Online] http://www.plannedparenthood.org (Accessed October 25, 1999)

Teen Challenge World Wide Network. [Online] http://www.teenchallenge.com (Accessed October 25, 1999)

4

Physical Fitness

Healthy living and physical fitness are closely connected. Being physically fit not only helps people live healthy lives, it also helps people live longer. People who make physical activity and exercise a part of their daily lives when they are young are more likely to keep it in their lives as they grow older and benefit from it throughout their lifespans. Physical activity is defined as any movement that spends energy. Exercise is a subset of physical activity, but it is an activity that is structured and planned.

While many children engage in physical activity, usually by playing with their friends, the amount of physical activity they get as they grow into adolescents usually declines. In fact, many researchers believe that physical inactivity is a national health problem that can increase the risk of illness and disease. According to the Centers for Disease Control and Prevention (CDC), doing some kind of physical activity or exercise on a regular basis helps to increase strength and flexibility, improve endurance, control weight, increase bone mass, and improve self-esteem, as well as reduce stress, anxiety, depression, and the risk of developing high blood pressure.

The best way to keep physical activity and exercise a permanent part of one's life is to make it fun and enjoyable. If people are given different options of what they can do and have easy access to those options, they are more likely to participate in physical activity and exercise. This allows people to have a positive attitude toward physical fitness. It's also helpful if people are knowledgeable about the rewards of physical activity and exercise.

This chapter will outline how physical activity and exercise benefit both the body and the mind in numerous ways. It will also discuss a number of different activity options, from team and individual sports, dancing, walking, gardening, and martial arts, to doing household chores and just playing with friends. Finally, it will explain the importance of setting goals, staying safe, and preventing injuries while keeping the body physically fit.

Benefits of Physical Activity and Exercise on the Body

Benefits of Physical Activity and Exercise on the Mind

Activities that Promote Fitness

How to Keep Physical Activity a Permanent Part of One's Life

BENEFITS OF PHYSICAL ACTIVITY AND EXERCISE ON THE BODY

It is a known fact that adding regular physical activity to one's daily routine will improve health and well-being. And that physical activity doesn't necessarily need to be strenuous for a person to enjoy benefits to health. Of course, by increasing the amount of physical activity (within reason), one will increase the amount of health benefits.

One of the most important benefits of physical activity is that it actually lessens a person's risk of developing or dying from many of the most common causes of serious illness and death in the United States. The risk of developing colon cancer, heart disease, high blood pressure, and diabetes is reduced through regular physical activity. Being physically active has also been proven to help build healthy bones, joints, and muscles. Furthermore, regular physical activity reduces the overall risk of dying prematurely from any cause. In fact, in 1995 the American College of Sports Medicine estimated that five times as many Americans die from being inactive than from losing their lives in car accidents.

Other benefits of physical activity and exercise include increased cardiovascular fitness, muscle strength, flexibility, energy, and bone mass.

WORDS TO KNOW

Aerobic: Something that occurs in the presence of oxygen.

Anaerobic: Something that occurs without oxygen because a person is using energy to do activities at a faster rate than the body is producing it.

Anxiety: Intense worry and fear.

Arthritis: Chronic inflammation of the joints.

Blood pressure: Pressure of blood against the walls of blood vessels.

Cardiovascular fitness: How efficiently the heart and lungs can pump blood (which holds oxygen) to muscles that are being worked.

Endorphins: Proteins in the brain that act as the body's natural pain reliever.

Endurance: A person's ability to continue doing a stressful activity for an extended period of time.

Exercise: A subset of physical activity, which is an activity that is structured and planned.

Heat stroke: A serious condition that causes the body to stop sweating and overheat dangerously.

Immune system: A body system that protects the body against illness.

Osteoporosis: A condition involving a decrease in bone mass, making bones more fragile.

Physical activity: Any movement that spends energy.

Stroke: A sudden loss of consciousness, feeling, and voluntary movement caused by a blood clot in the brain.

Tendinitis: Inflammation of a tendon.

Yoga: A series of exercises that incorporate regulated breathing, concentration, and flexibility.

Increase Cardiovascular Fitness

Regular activity and exercise make for a healthier heart. A healthy heart is a strong heart that works efficiently and is able to easily supply the body with blood. The heart pumps blood, which carries oxygen to muscles and carries away waste. How well the heart performs is a good indication of how healthy a person's cardiovascular (the heart and the blood vessels) system is.

Endurance refers to a person's ability to continue doing a stressful activity for an extended period of time. This is sometimes called stamina. What this means is that a person with good endurance or stamina can bike, jog, play, or run for a long time without getting tired. Having a healthy endurance level means that a person has a healthy level of cardiovascular fitness. Technically speaking, cardiovascular fitness refers to how efficiently the heart and lungs can pump blood (which holds oxygen) to muscles that are being worked. The more efficiently the heart works, the more energy the body has to continue working without a great deal of effort.

ACCORDING TO THE CENTERS FOR DISEASE CONTROL AND PREVENTION (CDC), NEARLY 50 PERCENT OF AMERICANS BETWEEN THE AGES OF TWELVE AND TWENTY-ONE DO NOT EXERCISE OR ENGAGE IN VIGOROUS PHYSICAL ACTIVITY ON A REGULAR BASIS.

Cardiovascular fitness is improved by aerobic exercise. The word aerobic refers to something that occurs in the presence of oxygen. Aerobic exercise improves cardiovascular health as it typically uses the body's largest groups of muscles (the legs) continually which makes a person need more oxygen. The more oxygen a person needs, the more efficiently his or her cardiovascular system must be functioning. Examples of aerobic exercise include running, walking fast, biking, and dancing. Incorporating cardiovascular, or aerobic, activity strengthens the heart and lungs. This makes it easier to do all sorts of everyday activities, such as hurrying to class, climbing stairs, or mowing the lawn.

Regular activity helps the cardiovascular system by improving circulation. Circulation is increased because physical activity increases a person's blood volume (amount). This makes it easier for the heart to function and more blood gets to muscles, meaning more oxygen is carried to the muscles. Exercise and activity also help reduce a person's chances of developing high blood pressure, or hypertension. Additionally, physical fitness reduces the risk of suffering a serious consequence, such as a stroke, from high blood pressure.

Gain Strength

Strength is the ability to resist force. Muscles constantly resist force. The more strength a person has, the easier it is for his or her muscles to resist greater force. For instance, someone who can lift one hundred pounds of weight once is stronger than someone who can lift fifty pounds of weight twice.

Just as regular physical activity builds strength, it also builds muscle endurance. Similar to cardiovascular endurance, muscle endurance means that muscles are able to work for longer periods of time, making it easier to swim another lap or carry a heavy knapsack while walking. Someone who can lift a fifty-pound dumbbell ten times has more muscular endurance than a person who can only lift that dumbbell once.

Many activities and exercises help to increase muscle strength. These are called anaerobic (without oxygen) because a person is using energy to do these activities at a faster rate than the body is producing it. Anaerobic

THE EVOLUTION OF EXERCISE IN ANCIENT TIMES

Some things never seem to change. People have been concerned with physical fitness for thousands of years. What does change is why people are concerned with fitness and what benefits they think being fit will bring them. Different cultures at various periods believed that physical activity and exercise would provide individuals, or even the government as a whole, with different attributes. These attributes provide insight into the evolution of exercise and activity as well as a view of what was valued by certain ancient cultures.

Preventing Illness in Ancient China

The martial art kung fu was developed in China over 4,000 years ago. There, people saw that individuals who were physically active on a regular basis didn't get sick as much as those who were inactive. Kung fu, then, was developed in order to help more people get exercise on a regular basis and avoid frequent illness.

Quieting the Mind in Ancient India

In ancient India, physical activities such as exercise and sports were not seen as being beneficial to the mind. Matters of the mind were of the utmost importance as far as Hindu and Buddhist priests were concerned. Yoga, a series of exercises that incorporate regulated breathing, concentration, and flexibility, became popular with disciplined Indians and priests, who used it as a method for emptying their minds of thoughts before meditating.

Preparing for Battle in Ancient Egypt and Ancient Persia

The link between a healthy body and a healthy mind was lost on the ancient Egyptians. Rather, they used physical activity and exercise primarily as a way to strengthen soldiers' bodies for warfare. Endurance exercises and the use of weapons were stressed. Likewise, the ancient Persians began training young males in warfare at very young ages, ignoring education, as having schooled soldiers was not deemed necessary to protecting Persia.

Perfecting the Body in Ancient Greece

People living in ancient Greece recognized that physical fitness was just as important as knowledge and learning. Ancient Greeks strove to be well-rounded individuals and, to them, that meant training the body and the mind. Furthermore, physical fitness was seen as its own reward. In fact, there weren't any professional competitions in which victors won valuable prizes. In the Olympic Games, which originated in ancient Greece, winners were awarded only a wreath fashioned out of olive branches.

Going for the Glory in Ancient Rome

Unlike the ancient greeks, ancient Romans valued physical fitness not just for its own merits but because it benefited the government. Physically fit men made better soldiers and workers, who helped protect and expand the empire. Ancient Romans preferred to witness the glory of a victor who had competed in professional games more than the humble victory of an amateur, who didn't reap material reward from a win.

activities include lifting heavy objects, doing chin-ups, or even taking out the trash.

Muscles grow through physical activity just as they can become more well-defined (in terms of appearance). Typically, however, more strenuous activity and exercise is required for this to occur. Muscle growth comes with activities and exercises that require strength, while muscle definition stems from exercises that require muscle endurance.

Stronger muscles go hand in hand with stronger bones and healthy joints. And, as the body builds muscle, it tends to lose fat, which results in a leaner, healthier body.

More strength means more activity can be done for a longer period of time.

Build Better Bones

Physical activity not only builds muscles, it builds stronger bones. The type of exercise that builds bones is weight-bearing or strength-bearing, such

THREE TYPES OF EXERCISE

Stretching, for flexibility

Weight-bearing, for strengthening muscles and bone mass

Aerobic, for the heart

Three types of physical activity: stretching and toning; muscle-building; and cardiovascular or aerobic. (Electronic Illustrators Group. Reproduced by permission of Gale Group.)

as playing baseball, soccer, tennis, walking, or weight-lifting. The bones that will be strengthened are those that are directly affected by the activity being done. This is why doing a variety of muscle-strengthening activities on a regular basis is important.

There are several reasons why weight-bearing activities build better bones. First, these activities seem to actually stimulate the formation of bone. Also, with physical activity comes muscle strength, which means that the muscles that are exerted grow stronger; this, in turn, benefits the bones. Finally, with improved strength, balance, and coordination, the risk of falls and bone injuries is greatly reduced.

Having thicker, healthier bones helps combat arthritis, a disease that involves the chronic inflammation of the joints, and osteoporosis later in life. Osteoporosis is a disease that gradually weakens bones, making them so fragile that they can fracture easily doing everyday activities. Osteoporosis takes time to develop, and many people are unaware that they have the disease until they fracture a bone. This can result in a painful, crippling condition that is irreversible. While it is true that osteoporosis mainly strikes older people, it is during childhood and adolescence that bones are forming. Building stronger bones during adolescence will help combat diseases such as osteoporosis later in life.

Breathe Easy

As people grow older, their lung capacity (how much air the lungs hold) grows smaller. Cardiovascular activity and exercise can combat this because aerobic activities actually increase lung capacity. So while lung capacity will continue to diminish because of age, with regular activity, especially aerobic activity, it will do so at a slower rate.

Boost Energy

Physical activity and exercise require energy, as does everything. In addition to expending energy, however, physical activity also gives people increased energy throughout the entire day.

The immune system, too, gets a big boost from regular physical activity. A healthy immune system helps fight colds, cancer, and other diseases, and speeds recovery from all kinds of injuries. The less time a person is ill, the more energy a person has to spend on living well.

To have energy to function, the human body needs sleep. Sleep, as does food, gives us energy. And regular physical activity helps people sleep more soundly. The more soundly one sleeps, the more energy one saves up during that time, and the more energy a person has to work, play, study, and do all sorts of things.

Improve Flexibility

Young people are usually quite flexible. But as with lung capacity, flexibility diminishes as people grow older. Activities and exercises that increase flexibility, such as gymnastics, martial arts, and yoga, are helpful in preventing injuries. The more flexible a person is, the less likely he or she is to suffer a sprain or strain a muscle while doing everyday things or while being active.

BENEFITS OF PHYSICAL ACTIVITY AND EXERCISE ON THE MIND

Physical activity and exercise are beneficial to the mind as well as the body. They help improve a person's health and overall outlook on life. In order to feel the best, have more energy, and stay healthy, a person should do something active at least three times a week. The great thing about physical activity and exercise is that it doesn't matter what a person does as long as it raises the heart rate for a certain period of time (twenty to thirty minutes is good); it is something one enjoys; and it is safe. This means that a person can bike, run, swim, or in-line skate, and each will help benefit the mind. Specifically, a person will experience a natural high and develop the ability to better handle emotions and changes in life.

Endorphins: The Natural High

When a person is physically active or exercises for a certain period of time—about 20 minutes or longer—the body releases endorphins, proteins in the brain that act as the body's natural pain reliever. When endorphins are released, a person may experience a feeling of euphoria. Many people enjoy this feeling and look forward to the natural high they get from keeping physically fit.

Improve Concentration

Concentration is important for learning and understanding new things and being able to perform well in all aspects of life. Being physically active and exercising can help improve concentration. This means that a person will be able to be more focused and perform better in class or during other activities. Staying physically fit has also been found to help people maintain mem-

EXERCISE IS FOR EVERYONE

Exercise benefits people of all ages. In addition, exercise is often more fun when done with friends or family. Being active with parents or grandparents is not just a great way to stay healthy, but it can be a time to bond with loved ones. Knowing that regular physical activity and exercise offer great benefits to aging adults is a good reason to make exercise a family affair. Muscle-strengthening activities reduce the risk of falling and fracturing bones. Increased activity equals increased bone strength, even in adults over ninety years old! As a person ages, physical activity can also decrease pain in joints from arthritis (a disease that causes inflammation of the joints).

ory longer in their lives. As people get older, their memory skills can deteriorate, and physical activity and exercise can help ward off this effect for some time.

Lift the Blues and Lower Anxiety

Many people suffer from depression and anxiety. A person may feel just depressed or anxious or experience both depression and anxiety at the same time. Depression can cause people to feel sad, tired, and/or hopeless, and suffer from low self-esteem. Anxiety causes feelings of panic. Both conditions can be treated by medication. But researchers have found that in mild cases, physical activity and exercise can help relieve feelings of depression and lower a person's anxiety.

Handle Stress Better

Stress is a normal part of every person's life. It is actually necessary to have some stress in life. Otherwise, a person would have no motivation for self-improvement or hard work. However, too much stress can cause many health problems. Some symptoms of stress include anxiety, high blood pressure, irritability, tense muscles, headaches, stomachaches, and lower resistance to illness. Physical activity and exercise, especially noncompetitive activity, help to manage stress. They give a person the opportunity to feel calmer and more alert, which can help a person work through the things that are causing the stress. They also boost the immune system, so resistance to illness will increase.

Build Self-Confidence and Self-Esteem

Low self-confidence and self-esteem can cause a person to engage in harmful behaviors, such as self-mutilation, drug addiction, or disordered eating. They may also seek acceptance from others in destructive ways, such as having sex before they're ready or drinking alcohol to excess. People with high self-confidence and self-esteem are usually happy with themselves, outgoing, and positive. They take pride in accomplishments and are able to stand up for themselves. They are not afraid of taking on new challenges and are not afraid of failure. Researchers have found that physical activity and exercise can increase self-confidence and self-esteem.

ACCORDING TO THE WOMEN'S SPORTS FOUNDATION, TEENS THAT PLAY SPORTS USUALLY DO NOT ENGAGE IN SEXUAL ACTIVITY UNTIL LATER IN LIFE AND ARE LESS LIKELY TO USE DRUGS OR BE INVOLVED IN ABUSIVE RELATIONSHIPS THAN TEENS WHO DO NOT PLAY SPORTS. THOSE STUDENTS WHO PLAY SPORTS ARE ALSO MORE LIKELY TO GRADUATE FROM HIGH SCHOOL AND COLLEGE.

Feel Calmer and Sleep Soundly

While physical activity and exercise can make people feel more alert during the day, they also allow people to feel calmer and sleep more soundly.

When people are active, their body temperature rises and warms their insides. This soothes the body, like a warm bath, and causes a person to feel calmer. This feeling, along with the lower anxiety and stress and physical benefits of physical activity and exercise, helps a person to sleep soundly at night.

ACTIVITIES THAT PROMOTE FITNESS

There are many types of activities that improve a person's physical fitness. The options range from traditional aerobics to alternative practices such as yoga and martial arts. Each activity has its own specific benefits and requires different kinds of equipment. Choosing the best activities involves finding the ones that are the most pleasurable and fun. The most important thing is doing some kind of activity on a regular basis.

Aerobic Exercise

Aerobic exercise strengthens the heart and lungs and tones the body. There are two types of aerobics: high-impact and low-impact. Both involve moving the body for at least twenty minutes in order to increase the heart rate to a point where the body is burning fat. High-impact aerobics involves dance combinations and jumping movements, while low-impact aerobics uses similar movements without the jumping. Low-impact aerobics is gentler to the joints because one foot is always touching the floor and therefore it is less likely to cause injury.

SPORTS AND THE MIND

Participation in sports—and other extracurricular activities such as band or dance troupes—is a great way of staying active, and sports offer wonderful rewards for mental health. Being involved in sports has been proven to help people learn valuable skills for dealing with life's ups and downs. They teach people how to interact with others and work as a team. This helps in daily life when working on a class project or a school play with others. Sports also help people become more independent and feel better about themselves. The result is positive self-esteem and self-confidence, which are extremely important to a person's happiness and success.

Sports also offer a fun and exciting environment in which to learn how to handle both failure and success. Everyone wins and loses at times in both sports and life. Winning feels great and empowering but can also cause a person to feel pressure and anxiety in the next attempt to win. Losing usually produces feelings of sadness, depression, and disappointment. Learning how to cope with these different feelings is important for good mental health.

Another aspect of sports that contributes to a healthy mind is goal-setting. People who have goals are more likely to be self-motivated and are usually able to accomplish more because they know what they need to do in order to get ahead. Without goals, people tend to lack direction and focus. In sports, goal-setting is essential for improving individually and working as a team. This is also true in life. For example, if a person wants to get better grades, accomplishing specific goals—such as studying for a certain period of time each night—is the fastest way to get those As.

A weekly aerobics class is a structured way of getting exercise. (Photograph (c) 1993 L. Steinmark. Custom Medical Stock Photo. Reproduced by permission.)

It's possible to get into aerobics through a class at a gym or recreation center as well as at home with a fitness video. Doing aerobics requires good sneakers for support and cool, comfortable clothing.

Biking

Biking is another fun activity that builds strength and balance. Riding for twenty minutes will make the heart strong and help the body burn fat. Most people learn to ride bikes as children, so all it takes to participate is a bicycle and road to ride it on. Some people choose to ride on the road, while others buy a mountain bike that allows them to ride on dirt roads and trails in the woods or in the mountains. In addition to having a bike, people need to wear helmets and have reflectors attached to the bike. Many people ride with friends or even join a cycling club to meet others who like to use their pedals to get their hearts pumping.

Boxing

Boxing tones and strengthens the whole body. Whether a person is just punching the air, called shadow boxing, or punching a bag, boxing helps burn fat, relieve stress, and increase endurance and confidence. People interested in boxing usually take classes at a local gym or learn boxing moves from a video. With boxing gloves and loose, comfortable workout clothing, boxing can be done at a gym, a recreation center, or at home. It's also possible to learn how to kick box, which uses the legs and the arms to punch the air or a bag.

Dance

Dance is great exercise for the whole body. It not only tones the body and burns fat, but it also improves balance and coordination. There are many different types of dance, including ballet, tap, modern, country-western, jazz, and hip-hop. Some people choose to take classes to learn the right technique. This can be especially important for tap and ballet. Others may rent or buy a video that teaches them the right moves. However, dance doesn't have to be structured. Dancing to a song on the radio or to a favorite CD is enough for some people. Dancing in any form is a fun way to become physically fit.

Dance classes are usually available at a private dance studio, a local community center, YMCA, or YWCA. It's necessary to have the proper shoes and sometimes the right clothing to take certain classes.

Gymnastics

Gymnastics is an intense activity that strengthens every muscle in the body. It also improves coordination and flexibility; however, it can be risky since many of the moves include flips and jumps that can cause injury. Practicing gymnastics requires classes at a gym with special equipment, a training camp, or a gymnastics clinic. It also requires an instructor, as gymnastic moves are difficult and cannot be learned without proper instruction. With the right clothing and a coach, a person can become involved with gymnastics for fitness. There is also rhythmic gymnastics, which combines dance and gymnastics and is generally less physically intense than traditional gymnastics.

Hiking

Hiking gives the legs and heart a good workout. Going up and down hills will strengthen the muscles in the thighs. Continuous hiking will increase the heart rate and burn fat. One of the best things about hiking is being surrounded by

KIDS AND EXERCISE

Physical activity and exercise are not the same. And while both are good for all people, most experts recommend that kids and preteens focus more on being physically active (such as playing or bike-riding) than on actually doing structured exercise (such as an aerobic exercise class). For example, the American Academy of Pediatrics recommends that weight training not be undertaken until after puberty and bone growth are complete.

Drawing of a man demonstrating the "single whip" sequence of tai chi. (Electronic Illustrators Group. Reproduced by permission of Gale Group.)

nature. Hiking trails can be found near beautiful mountains, giving hikers many choices of trails that differ in difficulty and scenery. Finding a place to hike, however, is not so easy for those who live in urban and suburban areas. Contacting the local parks and recreation department is the best way to find the closest hiking areas. Hikers need certain things to have a fun and safe time, including a good pair of hiking boots, socks, hat, water, sunscreen, food for energy, a few friends with whom to hike, and a trail map.

Ice Skating

On a frozen pond or in a rink, ice skating works the lower body, including thighs, hips, and buttocks. It also strengthens the heart, burns fat, and improves balance and coordination. Ice skating can be done without instruction, but in order to improve one's skating skills, lessons are a good idea. Individual and group lessons are available at local rinks. It's also possible to learn how to figure skate, which involves doing spins, jumps, and dance moves on the ice. Having a supportive pair of skates is essential. If there's nowhere to ice skate, but the activity is appealing, in-line skating is a great alternative.

In-Line Skating

In-line skating is similar to ice-skating but it's done on concrete, not ice. It works the lower body and strengthens the heart. In-line skating has grown in popularity over recent years and many people consider it to be one of the most fun activities to do. It can be done alone or with friends, and lessons are available at local parks or places where in-line skates are rented. Lessons can help people achieve more complicated moves and jumps. Getting involved means buying or renting a pair of skates, as well as wrist guards, elbow guards, kneepads, and a helmet for protection against falls and collisions.

The Martial Arts

The martial arts are a combination of physical activity and mental strength and development. The practice of the arts goes back thousands of years; they work to improve the body's strength, power, speed, endurance, control, balance, awareness, and timing. In addition to physical training, martial arts benefit the mind through meditation that brings peace of mind in daily life.

Figure skating champion Tara Lipinski took up ice skating at a young age. (Photograph by Denis Balibouse. Reuters/Archive Photos. Reproduced by permission.)

Classes are available in different types of martial arts at local studios or recreation centers. The different types of martial arts include karate, kung fu, aikido, judo, jujitsu, tae kwan do, and tai chi. A little research will help one find the right class. Participating in martial arts usually requires a martial arts uniform.

Playing

Playing is simple and fun, and anyone can do it. The options are endless and the benefits are great. Playing increases strength, flexibility, coordination, and muscle tone and, because it increases the heart rate, it burns fat as well. In addition to the physical benefits, playing relieves stress and gives the player a positive attitude about life and physical fitness. The types of playing activities include, but are not limited to, Frisbee, tag, hide-and-seek, raking and jumping in leaves, playing with a pet, gardening, and hopscotch. Playing can be done anytime and anywhere, alone or with friends. The only requirement is a lot of imagination.

Running

Running is an intense exercise. It's great for increasing heart rate, burning fat, and relieving stress. The muscles in the legs and stomach become stronger through running, and many runners talk of a "runner's high," which can be attributed to the release of endorphins, or the body's natural pain reliever, into the bloodstream. While most physical activity signals the body to produce endorphins, running causes the body to release more because of the intensity of the workout.

Cutting loose with friends is an easy and fun way to be active. (Photograph (c) 1992 Kevin Beebe. Custom Medical Stock Photo. Reproduced by permission.)

Not everyone is suited for running. The constant pounding on pavement can cause injuries, especially to knees and ankles. It's essential to have good running shoes with proper support and to run on soft surfaces whenever possible. Asphalt, dirt, grass, and sand are softer surfaces than concrete and are better for the body's joints. For those who are just starting, it's smart to begin slowly and increase speed and distance over many months. Running can be done alone, but it's often safer to run with a friend. And, while it can be done at any time, it's best to run when it's still light outside.

Skiing and Snowboarding

Downhill and cross-country skiing and snowboarding can be done only during the winter months, but they all have great physical benefits. Downhill skiing improves muscle tone for the whole body, as well as increasing balance and endurance. Cross-country skiing means constantly moving the arms and legs in a rhythmic fashion, which keeps the heart pumping fast. Snowboarding increases muscle tone in the lower body, while also improving balance and coordination.

Skiing and snowboarding take time to learn and require a lot of equipment that can be expensive. Equipment includes skis or a snowboard, special boots that can be rented or bought, warm clothing, a hat, and gloves. Most ski resorts offer lessons for all skill levels of skiers and snowboarders. Having access to these sports on a regular basis can be difficult, however, depending on where a person lives.

Swimming

Swimming is a fun activity that is easy on the body's joints because the water cushions the body while it moves. Swimming tones the whole body and increases the heart rate. It can be structured or unstructured. Doing laps with different types of strokes (backstroke or sidestroke, for example) is a possibility, as is just playing around in the water with friends or participating in a water volleyball game. It's difficult to swim year round, as most pools are outside and only open during the summer months. Some people have access to heated indoor pools, but they can be expensive. Still others go to the beach to swim in a lake or in the ocean. Swimming requires access to a pool or a beach, a bathing suit, and possibly goggles for doing laps. It is important that a person take structured swimming lessons before jumping into the water, however. Several

Swimming tones the whole body and increases the heart rate. (Photograph (c) 1992 T. McCarthy. Custom Medical Stock Photo. Reproduced by permission.)

skills, such as floating and proper breathing, must be mastered in order to ensure one's safety in the water.

Team Sports

Team sports offer a variety of benefits that are unique to each sport. Hockey, basketball, and soccer, for example, require constant movement and therefore are great for increasing the heart rate, burning fat, and toning muscle. They also improve coordination and endurance. Softball, baseball, football, and volleyball increase muscle strength and coordination. Track and field benefits the whole body as it can involve running, sprinting, jumping, and throwing. All team sports usually require the participant to train for the playing season.

Team sports provide a challenging, cooperative atmosphere and teach teamwork and mental concentration. It's possible to participate in more than

Girls' softball is a popular team sport in junior high schools and high schools.
(Photograph by Robert J. Huffman. Field Mark Publications. Reproduced by permission.)

one sport, depending on the seasons in which they are played. Most team sports are offered at school and through community programs. The school or community usually provides equipment although there may be a fee to cover the costs. Finding the right sport can depend on a person's skill level. Some teams require tryouts in order to join; however, some just look for enthusiasm and a good attitude in their players.

Tennis

Tennis can be played with two or four people or, in other words, singles or doubles. Either way provides a good workout, increasing strength in the arms and the legs, as well as improving eye-hand coordination. Singles is a more intense activity since one does not have a partner to help cover the court. Doubles can be more fun, however, because it involves more people and can be considered a social activity with friends. Both doubles and singles increase heart rate and burn fat, resulting in overall improved physical fitness. The game of tennis is competitive, which gives people a challenge and improves their mental skills of strategy and concentration.

ACCORDING TO THE CDC, AS KIDS GROW OLDER, THEIR LEVEL OF PHYSICAL ACTIVITY TENDS TO DECLINE.

Getting into tennis requires access to a court, a good racquet, and tennis shoes. Many communities have outside courts that people can use for free or for a small fee. During the winter months, there are indoor courts that can be used, but they are usually more expensive. Some people take lessons to improve their skills. Most tennis centers and clubs offer classes for different skill levels. They may also offer tournaments where people compete with others at the same skill level.

Walking

Walking is one of the most simple and accessible activities. Most people do some walking every day. Going for a fast, long walk, sometimes called power walking, will increase heart rate and burn fat, while also improving endurance. Walking uphill will increase muscle tone in the legs, back, stomach, and buttocks. Pumping the arms while walking will tone the arms and shoulders. Walking can be done anywhere, alone or with friends. (For safety's sake, it is best to walk in well-lit areas or with a friend.) It's also a great stress reliever. The only requirement is a good pair of walking shoes. If the weather isn't nice, some people choose to walk indoors on a treadmill at a gym or they head to their local mall.

Yoga

Yoga is a way of life that connects the mind, body, and spirit. Through different poses, or postures, yoga improves flexibility, strength, circulation, and relieves stress while helping a person achieve peace of mind. Yoga will also improve the body's alignment, which means all the body's parts are in the right position for good health. There are many different types of yoga that a person can practice. It can be done at home with the help of an instruction book or a video. It's also possible to take yoga classes at a local gym or community center. All a person needs is comfortable clothing, an exercise mat, and an open mind. [*See also* Chapter 10: Alternative Medicine for more information on yoga.]

HOW TO KEEP PHYSICAL ACTIVITY A PERMANENT PART OF ONE'S LIFE

Set Goals

Setting goals for staying physically fit is important. These goals can be as small as making sure to do some kind of activity three times a week and as large as wanting to join the ski team. The key to successful goal-setting is making small goals that can be achieved daily and when added up can equal the accomplishment of a long-term goal. For example, if a person wants to start playing basketball, he or she can start with the short-term goal of shooting baskets with friends every week. The long-term goal may be to join the basketball team at school.

BE REALISTIC. When setting goals, a person should pay attention to how realistic the goals are. It doesn't make sense for a person to focus on trying to be a successful surfer if one doesn't live near water. Nor is it good for someone who is currently inactive to suddenly try to take up long-distance running. This will only lead to frustration. It's smart to take smaller steps in the quest for fitness, based on a person's schedule, skill, and access to different kinds of activities.

MAKE SOME GOALS CHALLENGING. Making realistic goals does not mean making only easy goals. Some should be challenging. This will increase feelings of accomplishment when the challenging goals are met. Challenging goals will also help maintain interest in one or more activities. Anything can become boring after awhile. By tossing in some challenges, interest and enjoyment will remain high. Challenging goals will also allow someone to improve his or her skill at an activity.

EXTREME SPORTS

Extreme sports are becoming more and more popular among young people. They offer the thrill of facing difficult challenges and overcoming obstacles. Extreme sports get the heart racing and put the body and mind to the test in the face of danger. With the many physical and mental benefits of extreme sports comes the risk of injuries. It's essential to work with a trained instructor and use the necessary safety equipment when doing any kind of extreme sport.

Extreme sports are not for everyone. However, those looking for bigger challenges in their quest for physical fitness have many options, including rock and ice climbing, surfing, whitewater rafting, wakeboarding, water-skiing, mountain-bike racing, bicycle stunt-riding, skydiving, skateboarding, and extreme snowboarding. There are many camps around the country that teach extreme sports to kids and teenagers. Anyone can find the nearest extreme sports camp or more general information by typing "extreme sports" on any Internet search engine. There are thousands of websites devoted to these exciting activities.

STICK WITH IT! Being active should be a lifelong pursuit. The human body is made to move, and when it doesn't, it suffers. Goals should be assessed every so often to make sure they are still important in one's life. The goals that are no longer important should be changed. A person's interests change throughout life and so should goals. As goals are met, new ones should be established, and a person should remember to reward him- or herself after successfully completing a goal.

Keeping Fitness Fun and Safe

GET A CHECK-UP. Being fit involves physical activity and exercise as well as a good diet. A person who is just starting to become more active should start slowly. Also, before anyone starts to become more active than usual, a complete check-up from a physician is necessary. This will help a person

A young man shows off his skills at an extreme bike-riding exhibition. (Photograph by Robert J. Huffman. Field Mark Publications. Reproduced by permission.)

learn how to be active if there is an existing health condition or injury, as well as be aware of how much one can and cannot do.

GUARD AGAINST INJURY. As important as it is to be physically active, it's also important to stay safe while being active. The first step in keeping fitness safe is wearing proper equipment. When playing on the street, biking, running, or in-line skating in the evening or on overcast days, reflective gear should be worn. Protective gear, which may include helmets, elbow and wrist guards, and gloves depending on the activity, are all necessary for biking, in-line skating, and for extreme sports, such as snowboarding.

FRIENDS MAKE IT FUN. Whenever possible, it is always safest to play or do physical activities with friends. Some activities and sports require that they be done by more than one person, such as basketball or street hockey. Other activities, such as biking, running, doing gymnastics, or walking can be and often are done alone. This is okay as long as these activities are carried out in safe, well-lit places. Isolated places, such as empty parks or roads,

Whether running or practicing yoga, Madonna works out faithfully. (Photograph by Kathy Willens. AP/Wide World Photos. Reproduced by permission.)

KEEPING THE FAITH
WITH RAY KYBARTAS

Ray Kybartas is a fitness trainer who helps teach others how to keep fitness a part of every-day life. His most famous client is pop star Madonna. In an introduction for Kybartas's 1997 book *Fitness Is Religion: Keep the Faith,* Madonna relates that during her first workout with Kybartas she realized "it was possible to exercise and enjoy yourself." She also points out, "There are no rules. All you need is dedication," and that "the goal has been much more about peace of mind than having a perfect body."

Kybartas's philosophy about fitness, which has greatly influenced Madonna, is that it should be a way of life. Like religion, Kybartas writes, fitness requires a lifelong commitment. This commitment will result in better health, both physically and mentally. A lifelong pursuit of fitness may seem daunting or overwhelming, but, according to Kybartas, once the commitment is made, most people look forward to being physically active and exercising on a regular basis because it makes them feel so good. One of Kybartas's suggestions for keeping fitness in your life is "doing something you enjoy . . . . If you want to walk, run, dance, row, swim, cycle, in-line skate, cross-country ski, practice yoga—whatever—then do it."

can leave a person at risk for many dangers. Taking familiar paths when walking or running and doing activities with other people around lessens danger from strangers. It also makes it easier to get help quickly if an injury occurs. A person taking a walk or going for a jog should let others know where he or she is headed.

TALK TO A PRO. Before anyone gets involved in an exercise such as weight training, a professional trainer should be consulted. This will assure that a person is using proper form and following a healthy training program. The same is true for extreme sports, such as snowboarding and rock climbing. This is because these activities usually involve a certain degree of danger and require safety equipment and training.

Beach volleyball, basketball, or street hockey are easy games to throw together with just a few friends. (Photograph by Robert J. Huffman. Field Mark Publications. Reproduced by permission.)

Dangers of Too Much Exercise

physical fitness

There are wonderful rewards for exercising: physical fitness and good mental health. However, a person can exercise too much and cause health problems. Some athletes are even dying from exercising too long and hard. Everyone should be aware of the dangers of exercise when beginning or maintaining a physical fitness program.

GIVE YOUR BODY A REST. A body is not made to be on the go all the time. It needs to rest. While exercise is good, it does tire the body. Overdoing exercise can result in feeling tired, weak, sore, or irritable. A person shouldn't exercise more than six days a week. If one feels tired or sore during or after being physically active, those are signals to rest.

OVERHEATING. Like a car, bodies can overheat. It is easy to overheat if a person is active on a hot day. A person should try not to exercise outside in very high temperatures. If one does, one should drink a lot of water, wear well-ventilated clothing, and pay attention to how the body is reacting to the heat.

Overheating should not be ignored. The symptoms of overheating can include cramps, nausea, tingling and clammy skin, and can lead to heat exhaustion or heat stroke. Signs of heat exhaustion include sweating a lot, skin that is clammy and cool, and a pulse that is rapid and weak. It is important for anyone experiencing these symptoms to get out of the heat, lie down, and drink water. Heat stroke is a more serious condition that causes the body to stop sweating and overheat dangerously. A person will feel confused and dizzy, and the skin will become red, dry, and hot. Medical attention is necessary for anyone who suffers from heat stroke. As soon as it starts, a person should stop exercising, get out of the heat, and drink water.

DON'T PUMP UP THE VOLUME TOO MUCH!

Walkmans and other portable radio and CD-players are very popular with people who are physically active. While getting into shape, they listen along to their favorite tunes. Music can help motivate people into walking a bit farther, playing a bit longer, or pushing themselves just a tiny bit harder. However, when a portable radio is played too loudly, a person may not hear what is being said or done around her, such as a person yelling or a car beeping its horn. It is important, then, to keep the volume low enough so that one is aware of his surroundings, which can prevent injury and lessen the threat of danger from strangers.

INJURIES. Exercising too much can cause injuries. It is easy to worsen slight injuries if a person doesn't pay attention to soreness or pain. As soon as a person experiences discomfort while exercising, he or she should stop and the injured area should be rested. Time should be taken for the injured area to heal before exercising again. However, depending on the seriousness of the injury, a person may continue to exercise as long as the focus is on exercising other parts of the body. For example, if the injury is in the shoulder, a person may jog or skate to avoid using the shoulder. Working different areas of the body on different days is helpful in properly resting the body throughout a fitness program.

Sweating while exercising is normal; sweating profusely, however, may be a sign one is overdoing it. (Photograph (c) Lee F. Snyder. Photo Researchers, Inc. Reproduced by permission.)

Some common injuries associated with exercise and sports include strains, sprains, shin splints, stress fractures, tendinitis, tennis elbow, and runner's knee. Strains occur when muscles or tendons (tissue that attaches muscles to bones) tear as they are stretched beyond their limit, and sprains happen when ligaments (tissue that holds bones together) are stretched too far or torn. Shin splints, or pain along the shin, occur when muscles along the shin are damaged, and stress fractures, or small cracks in bones, may happen when bones are stressed by intense exercise. Inflammation of a tendon is called tendinitis. This condition commonly affects the tendons in the hands, upper arm, or heel.

Some injuries, such as tennis elbow and runner's knee, have names that are associated with the sport in which the injury is common. However, one can still suffer from tennis elbow or runner's knee even if one is not a tennis player or runner. Tennis elbow occurs when tendons at the elbow are damaged. Tendons that move the wrist either forward or backward may be affected. Runner's knee is when the kneecap, which normally moves up and down during movement without touching another bone, rubs against the end of the thigh bone as a person walks or runs.

To help prevent injuries, a person should always warm up before exercising and cool down afterward. Warming up means starting out slow for the first ten minutes of exercise. This allows blood flow to increase in the muscles, which warms up the muscles and makes them more flexible. Cooling down means slowing down gradually after exercising. This will let blood flow from the areas that were being worked to other parts of the body, especially the head, which will reduce the chance of dizziness or fainting following a hard workout. A proper cool-down will also help keep muscles from getting too stiff.

Another way of helping to prevent injury is for a person to vary the kinds of physical activity he or she does. This allows different parts of the body to be used so the same parts are not always being stressed. Also, more parts of the body will get stronger, which will contribute to total body fitness. [*See also* Chapter 8: Preventive Care.]

EXERCISE ADDICTION. Looking forward to exercise and feeling good about the effects of exercise on the body is normal. Exercise feels great and provides people with more energy and increases self-esteem. However, some people use exercise as a way to purge the body of calories to try to become thinner. This is considered an eating disorder. People who suffer from exercise addiction, or compulsive exercising, are not exercising to become physically fit. Instead, they are exercising to try to obtain the ideal body shape. However, the ideal body shape is an unrealistic and impossible goal.

Every person is born with a certain genetic makeup that will determine one's body shape. If the body that a person is striving for is not possible, that person will be disappointed and most likely engage in unhealthy behavior, such as improper dieting and overexercising. The best approach to exercise is to use it to become physically fit and maintain health. This approach will produce the body shape that is right for each person. [*See also* exercise addiction section in Chapter 13: Eating Disorders.]

WHAT IS R.I.C.E.?

R.I.C.E. is a suggested way of treating most exercise- or sports-related injuries. Each letter stands for a certain part of treatment.

Rest. Rest gives an injury time to heal.

Ice. Ice should be applied to an injury in order to relieve pain and swelling.

Compression. A bandage should be wrapped around an injury for support and to help limit swelling.

Elevation. The injured area should be elevated to keep fluid from collecting there.

If the pain or swelling is intense, a person should seek medical attention.

FOR MORE INFORMATION

Books

Cohen, Neil, ed. *The Everything You Want to Know About Sports Encyclopedia: A* Sports Illustrated for Kids *Book.* New York: Bantam Books, 1994.

Kybartas, Ray. *Fitness Is Religion: Keep the Faith.* New York: Simon and Schuster, 1997.

Nardo, Don. *Exercise.* New York: Chelsea House Publishers, 1992.

Scwager, Tina and Michele Schuerger. *The Right Moves: A Girl's Guide to Getting Fit and Feeling Good.* Minneapolis, Minn.: Free Spirit Publishing, 1998.

Web Sites

American School Health Association. [Online] http://www.ashaweb.org (Accessed October 20, 1999).

Centers for Disease Control and Prevention. [Online] http://www.cdc.gov (Accessed October 20, 1999).

Kid's Health. [Online] http://www.kidshealth.org (Accessed October 20, 1999).

National Association for Sport and Physical Education. [Online] http://www.aahperd.org/naspe.html (Accessed October 20, 1999).

President's Council on Physical Fitness and Sports. [Online] http://www.dhhs.gov/progorg/ophs (Accessed October 20, 1999).

5

Environmental Health

Environmental health is a two-way street. Our environment, in the largest sense, is the complex network of physical, chemical, biological, and ecological components that make up the natural world. How clean and unpolluted the air, water, and soil of this environment are can affect the health of human beings. On the other hand, the way people treat the environment in their professional, industrial, and recreational activities helps determine how clean and safe it will be. In short, the environment affects the health of human beings, and human beings affect the health of the environment. All of the issues that evolve out of the interaction between people and the environment fall under the umbrella of environmental health.

Governments, companies, and individuals have a responsibility to preserve and promote environmental health. Government agencies, like the Environmental Protection Agency (EPA), founded in 1970, regulate industry to limit pollution that can damage the environment. The EPA's mission is to protect public health and the quality of the natural environment. Legislation like the Clean Air Act, passed by Congress in 1970, protects air quality by setting standards of purity for the air circulated in homes, schools, and workplaces. Groups outside the government, such as the World Wildlife Foundation, also work to identify and control threats to the environment that will endanger the food, water, and homes of plants and animals.

Everyone must make choices about how and where to live. Whether people are watching television in their living rooms, working at an office, eating at a restaurant, swimming at a beach, bicycling in a park, or sitting in a classroom, they should be aware of the condition of the environment around them. Good environmental health means having a safe, clean environment so that everyone can be healthy and productive within it. This chapter discusses the many different risks that threaten the environment, including radiation, pesticides, and indoor and outdoor air pollution, as well as ways to protect the environment and those who live in it.

Radiation

Pesticides

Outside Air Pollution

Indoor Air Pollution

Endocrine Disrupters

environmental
health

Radiation is energy, or emission of energy, in the form of waves or particles. Microscopic particles, called atoms, are the foundation on which all matter (all substances that exist as solids, liquids, or gas) is built. Each atom has a nucleus at its center. The nucleus contains smaller (nuclear) particles called protons and neutrons. If the number, position, or energy level of these nuclear particles changes, an atom becomes unstable, or radioactive. Unstable atoms, or atoms undergoing change, produce radiation.

Sources of Radiation

Radiation is everywhere. It occurs naturally in soil and water on Earth. It exists in outer space and inside human bodies. Since the natural sources exist everywhere, these sources are sometimes called background radiation. There are human-made sources of radiation, too. Radiation has been harnessed for use in science, medicine, and industry. X-ray technology, nuclear power plants, and some forms of electricity use radiation. According to the United States Environmental Protection Agency (EPA), 80 percent of radiation sources are natural and 20 percent are synthetic (human-made).

Types of Radiation: Non-ionizing and Ionizing Radiation

Two major types of radiation are non-ionizing radiation and ionizing radiation. Non-ionizing radiation is the less potent (strong) form. It has the power to move atoms around, but not to chemically change (or ionize) them. Ionizing radiation, on the other hand, does have the power to chemically

WORDS TO KNOW

Acid rain: Rain with a high content of sulfuric acid.

Asbestos: A mineral fiber.

Byproduct: Something other than the main product that is produced in a chemical or biological process.

Carbon monoxide: A colorless, odorless, tasteless gas that turns into carbon dioxide when it is burned.

Carcinogenic: Cancer-causing.

Contaminate: To infect something or make something unsafe for use.

Cosmic: Relating to the universe in contrast to Earth.

Emission: Substances released into the air.

Endocrine disrupter: Manmade chemical that looks and acts like naturally-occurring hormones.

Environmental tobacco smoke (ETS): The mixture of the smoke from a lit cigarette, pipe, or cigar and the smoke exhaled by the person smoking; also known as secondhand smoke.

Herbicide: A chemical agent used to kill damaging plants, such as weeds.

Incinerator: A machine that burns waste materials.

Industrial: Relating to a company that manufactures a product.

Inert: A chemical agent lacking in active properties.

Leaching: The process of dissolving outward by the action of a permeable substance.

Lead: A heavy, flexible, metallic element that is often used in pipes and batteries.

change atoms and it is this power that makes it a threat to humans and the environment. There are three major types of ionizing radiation. They are called alpha, beta, and gamma rays. (They can also be described as radioactive particles, or radiation.) Each of these sub-groups is distinguished from the others by the ease or difficulty with which it can penetrate (or enter) the human body.

ALPHA RADIATION. The ability of an alpha particle to enter the body can be blocked by paper or skin, but alpha particles can enter the body through an open wound and do harm. Airborne alpha particles that are inhaled can cause serious lung damage.

BETA RADIATION. Paper cannot block beta radiation from entering the body. Some beta particles would be deterred by skin, while still more powerful beta particles would require something the thickness of wood to prevent entry. If beta rays do find their way into the body, they can get into the bones and cause damage.

GAMMA RADIATION. Gamma rays are the most powerful particles. Often appearing along with alpha and beta rays, these dangerous rays can

COMMON SOURCES OF RADIATION TO WHICH PEOPLE CAN BE EXPOSED

- computer terminal
- cosmic rays from outer space
- ingested food and water containing elements like potassium
- medical X ray
- radiation in cancer treatment
- radon gas (in the air)
- rocks and soil
- smoke detector
- television
- X-ray luggage inspection machine

Microscopic: Invisible without the use of a microscope, an instrument that enlarges images of tiny objects.

Nitrogen dioxide: A gas that cannot be seen or smelled. It irritates the eyes, ears, nose, and throat.

Ozone layer: The atmospheric shield that protects the planet from harmful ultraviolet radiation.

Particle: A miniscule pollutant released when fuel does not burn completely.

Pesticide: A chemical agent used to kill bugs.

Potassium: A chemical element that is a silver-white, soft metal occurring in nature.

Radiation: Energy or rays emitted when certain changes occur in the atoms or molecules of an object or substance.

Radon: A colorless, odorless, radioactive gas produced by the naturally occurring breakdown of the chemical element uranium in soil or rocks.

Sulfur dioxide: A toxic gas that can also be converted to a colorless liquid.

Synthetic: Something that is man-made; not found in nature

Thyroid: A gland that controls the growth of the body

Toxic: Relating to or caused by a poison

Uranium: A chemical element that is a silver-white, hard metal and is radioactive.

Volatile organic compound (VOC): An airborne chemical that contains carbon.

break through paper, skin, and wood. A concrete wall would be needed to deflect gamma rays. If gamma rays penetrate the body, they can cause major damage to internal organs.

Radiation Risks

Most scientists agree that radiation can be carcinogenic (cancer-causing); indeed, the major health risk radiation poses is an increased risk of developing cancer. Other harmful effects that have been observed include genetic abnormalities in the children of parents who had significant exposure to radiation. Mental retardation, in particular, has been observed in children whose mother was exposed to a significant amount of radiation.

EXPOSURE TO RADIATION, OR THE DOSE (AMOUNT) OF EXPOSURE, IS MEASURED BY A UNIT CALLED A REM. THE UNIT OF MEASURE FOR SMALLER DOSES IS THE MILLIREM. A REM IS EQUAL TO 1,000 MILLIREMS. ACCORDING TO EPA SCIENTISTS, AN AVERAGE U.S. CITIZEN'S ANNUAL RADIATION EXPOSURE IS ABOUT 360 MILLIREMS PER YEAR.

Exposure to radioactive elements in the ground, such as thorium and potassium, can vary depending on where a person lives since the composition of land varies in different places. Exposure from cosmic radiation that is discharged into the atmosphere from outer space can also vary by location. Places that are at a higher elevation have thinner atmospheres and less protection from

A radon test kit for the home. (Photograph by Robert J. Huffman. Field Mark Publications. Reproduced by permission.)

RADON AND ITS THREAT TO HUMAN LIFE

While cosmic rays represent some 8 percent of human exposure to natural radiation, EPA scientists suggest that radon accounts for an overwhelming 55 percent of human exposure to natural sources of radiation.

Produced by the decay of radioactive uranium (a chemical element) widely found in soils around the planet, radon gas has no color, taste, or odor. Radon travels up from the ground to seep into the foundation of a school, home, or other building. Once inside a building, airborne radon can become a threat to human health. If unhealthy amounts of radon are inhaled, it can damage the lungs and cause lung cancer. Scientists believe radon is second only to smoking as a cause of lung cancer, with thousands of lung cancer deaths in America each year thought to be the result of radon exposure.

cosmic radiation. Locations that are closer to sea level have a bigger buffer zone and are less susceptible to cosmic radiation.

The Food and Drug Administration (FDA) and EPA insure that strict guidelines are followed for medical procedures involving radiation. The personnel, equipment, and facilities involved all have to meet certain standards to insure that radiation is managed as safely as possible. The Nuclear Regulatory Committee (NRC) has made tougher rules to govern construction, maintenance, emissions, and operations of nuclear power plants to decrease the risk of dangerous nuclear accidents. Stronger rules have also been developed for disposal of the radioactive waste, which is the byproduct of medical, scientific, and industrial uses of radiation.

What to Do About Radiation Exposure

Even with federal agencies monitoring radiation risks and working to control dangerous exposure to human populations and the environment, people still can't avoid radiation altogether. But precautions can be taken to limit exposure. When doctors recommend getting an X ray, people should not be afraid to take a few moments to talk about the risks versus benefits. Also, people in any community should be encouraged to get homes or schools tested to find out if the radon levels are acceptable.

There are three key strategies to limiting radiation exposure:

1. Time spent near an identified source of radiation should be limited.

2. Distance from an identified source of radiation should be kept; more distance means less exposure.

3. Identified sources of radiation should be shielded, keeping them out of or away from the body where they can do damage; for example, cracks in pipes and foundations should be repaired to block radon from getting into the air of homes.

Concerns about radiation in one's environment can be addressed by writing to state legislators to find out what is being done to correct or prevent a problem. Individuals can stay up to date on environmental issues so as to know what the latest studies say about sources of radiation in the everyday environment, such as computers and television. More information helps to make smarter choices about what to do, or not do, to limit exposure to dangerous sources or levels of radiation.

FEDERAL AGENCIES WORKING TO LIMIT RADIATION EXPOSURE

Environmental Protection Agency (EPA)

Nuclear Regulatory Committee (NRC)

Department of Health and Human Services (HHS)

Department of Energy (DOE)

Department of Defense (DOD)

Department of Transportation (DOT)

Occupational Safety and Health Administration (OSHA)

Human beings rely on a wide range of plants and animals for food. The majority of what people eat is grown or raised on the land, or from the waters, around the Earth. Plants or animals that interfere with or destroy human agricultural or livestock efforts are called pests. Animals, particularly insects and rodents, that can cause damage to human homes, lawns, food, and sanitation are also called pests. Pesticides are the products, usually chemically based, that are used to fight or kill these pests.

Common Types of Pesticides

Pesticides are used in agriculture on a large scale. Powerful chemical agents that deter a harmful weed or pest might be sprayed over large areas

Each day people are exposed to low levels of radiation by such things as TVs and computers. (Photograph by Robert J. Huffman. Field Mark Publications. Reproduced by permission.)

of crops. On a smaller scale, individuals use pesticides to protect their homes and yards. Pesticide products can be bought in many forms including sprays, liquids, sticks, powders, crystals, balls, and foggers. Products that are commonly used to control pests around the house include insecticides (insects), termiticides (termites), rodenticides (rodents), fungicides (fungi, such as mold), and disinfectants (germs that can cause disease).

Pros and Cons of Pesticide Use

The use of pesticides is surrounded by controversy. Pesticides serve an invaluable function in protecting the crops and livestock that are vital to people's food supply. Pesticides can also help defend people's homes against germs and unsanitary and destructive pests. On the other hand, some pesticides contain and spread chemicals, which are toxic (poisonous), or even fatal, if they are consumed by human beings.

Each pesticide contains an active chemical ingredient that is targeted to kill a specific plant or animal pest. But these ingredients are surrounded, or carried, by chemical agents referred to as inerts. They are called inert (meaning lacking in active properties) because they do not have an active effect on the targeted pest. The problem is that inerts can be toxic to other animals or plants with which they come into contact. Some of these inerts are so toxic that, to insure public safety, the recommended usage of the pesticide is limited to mere ounces per acre of land.

Pesticide Risks in Agriculture

Although pesticides are a relatively cost-effective way to protect crops and livestock from damage or destruction, the potential health risks (and the costs that might be generated by them) also need to be considered. Aerial (air) or ground applications of pesticides are hard to control because herbicides (chemical agents used on damaging plants, such as weeds) can drift onto unintended areas.

Methods used to try to control this drift include applying pesticides closer to the ground; waiting for wind to be at a minimum when spraying; using spray nozzles that tightly focus the outgoing stream of pesticides; and adding thick-

CONTROLLING PESTICIDE USE

The Federal Insecticide, Fungicide, and Rodenticide Act (FIFRA) was passed in 1947 to establish more controls over pesticide use. In 1972, the Federal Environmental Pest Control amendment further expanded standards for products and procedures used in pest management. This amendment introduced the following controls:

- It is illegal to use pesticides in an amount or manner other than what is specified on the product label.

- There will be heavy fines and/or imprisonment for improper pesticide use.

- There must be a distinction between general-use and restricted-use pesticides.

- State certification is required for restricted-use pesticides.

- Environmental Protection Agency (EPA) is required to investigate pesticide manufacturing plants.

- Registration is required of all pesticides by the EPA.

- Scientific research is required to confirm a product's effectiveness on killing targeted pests and to confirm no risks to people, other plants, and other animals (assuming the product is used as directed).

eners to pesticides to help focus active ingredients toward the intended targets. Pesticide users also have to be careful to remove contamination from the sprayers before using them again. Tobacco, grapes, tomatoes, garden vegetables, and fruit trees are particularly vulnerable to certain pesticides used on other crops. The remains left in a sprayer from a previously used pesticide can harm these crops.

The federal government has set standards that the workers, equipment, and procedures involved with pesticide use in industrial agriculture have to meet. These standards help to protect workers, crops and livestock, and the public—the ultimate consumers of the food—from the health risks of pesticide contamination or exposure.

Organic (natural) farming methods do not involve the use of chemical-based pesticides. (Photograph by Robert J. Huffman. Field Mark Publications. Reproduced by permission.)

Protection from Pesticides

There are steps everyone can take to protect against the known (and potential) health risks of pesticide use or exposure.

- After pesticide is used on an area, it must be aired out.
- One can investigate and use non-chemical alternatives to pesticides.
- Pest control companies should be screened before being hired to work in the home.
- Pesticides must be stored carefully.
- Pesticides must be disposed of properly.
- Pesticides must not be applied or disposed of in streams or areas where wildlife drink and feed. (Waste can travel so it's important to be aware not only of the immediate location, but the areas and waterways it might be connected to, or drain into.)
- The Internet, science teachers, and the media can help to keep the public educated and updated on environmental issues.

OUTSIDE AIR POLLUTION

A major concern of environmental health is the quality of the air people breathe. There are both natural and synthetic processes that decrease air quality, or cause air pollution. Following is a breakdown of some of the major areas of concern.

Acid Rain

Beginning in the 1970s, there has been growing concern about the problem of acid rain. Acid rain is rain with a high content of sulfuric acid, which is produced when sulfur dioxide combines with hydrogen. Sulfur dioxide is released from natural sources, such as volcanoes, sea spray, and rotting vegetation. Burning fossil fuels such as coal and oil also produces it. Once released, the sulfuric acid mixes with hydrogen, a gas that is already in the atmosphere. The resulting sulfuric acid falls back down to the earth as a pollutant, acid rain.

Acid rain poses health risks to people and nature. The danger for people is respiratory (breathing) problems such as asthma, dry coughs, headache, and eye/ear/nose/throat irritations. Another danger of acid rain is that it contains the remains of toxic metals. When acid rain falls, toxic remains can be absorbed by fruits, vegetables, and livestock and passed on to human consumers. Consumption of these toxic metals, such as mercury for example, can lead to brain damage, kidney problems, and even death.

The sulfuric acid in acid rain is a particular threat to forests and soils. Sulfuric acid competes with trees for vital nutrients, limits their hardiness to withstand cold temperatures, and triggers unhealthy growing cycles. Sulfuric acid also has a corrosive, or damaging, effect on buildings and statues.

VOCs (volatile organic compounds)

In science, something that can easily become airborne is called volatile. Chemicals that contain carbon, a fundamental element of all living organisms, are called organic. Volatile organic compounds (VOCs) are elements with both of these features.

VOCs are released when fuel, including gasoline, oil, wood, coal, and natural gas, is burned. They are also found in commonly used solvents, paints, and glues. The exhaust from cars is a big source of VOCs.

VOCs have been linked to serious health risks, such as cancer, but they are known mostly for their role in forming smog. Smog is a chemical haze, or fog, that is made heavier and darker by smoke and chemical fumes. It occurs when ultraviolet radiation from the sun comes into contact with atmospheric pollution.

Carbon Monoxide

Carbon monoxide is a colorless, odorless, tasteless gas that turns into carbon dioxide when it is burned. Produced by burning gasoline, natural gas, coal, oil, or other materials, carbon monoxide cripples the flow of oxygen to cells and tissues that cannot function without it. People who suffer from respiratory or circulatory problems are especially vulnerable to health problems from exposure to carbon monoxide.

Sulfur Dioxide

Sulfur dioxide is a toxic gas that can also be converted to a colorless liquid. It is produced when coal, oil, or sulfur is burned. A key ingredient in sulfuric acid, sulfur dioxide is also used in processes such as bleaching, preservation, and refrigeration. It is used heavily in generating paper and metal. Sulfur dioxide ranks as one of the most significant causes of air pollution, particularly in industrial areas.

Lead

Lead is a heavy, flexible metallic element that is often used in pipes and batteries. It is also

A young girl displays lead paint chips that have been scraped from old playground equipment. (Photograph by Robert J. Huffman. Field Mark Publications. Reproduced by permission.)

an ingredient in some gasoline and paint. Sources of lead in the environment include leaded gasoline, house and car paint, metal refineries (smelters), and the production of lead storage batteries. Lead can cause severe damage to the human brain or nervous system, particularly in children. It can also cause digestive problems, and some chemicals that contained lead have been shown to cause cancer in animals.

Lead-based paint can lead to serious health problems. Dust and chips can crack off the paint in tiny particles, but even a small amount of lead ingested into the system of a child or pregnant woman can have a serious impact. If a child swallows or inhales lead, it can cause learning disabilities and disorders of the nervous system. Adults who ingest high levels of lead may experience high blood pressure, headaches, digestive problems, pain in joints and muscles, and other health problems. In 1978, lead-based paint was banned because of the threat to public health, but homes and schools built before 1978 may still have lead-based paint in or on them. Lead-based gasoline is also in the process of being phased out.

Environmental Effects of Outside Air Pollution

According to the Environmental Protection Agency (EPA), 60 to 70 U.S. metropolitan areas—that are home to some 62 million Americans—do not meet air quality standards for one or more air pollutants. Total emissions of nitrogen oxides (NOx) that are thought to damage the environment have increased by 14 percent since 1970. Cars and power plants are large contributors to this problem. Chemicals that threaten the Earth's ozone layer (the atmospheric shield that protects the planet from harmful ultraviolet radiation) are another concern. If the integrity of the ozone layer is compromised, the Earth will be exposed to ultraviolet radiation and this could result in increases in the occurrence of skin cancer and cataracts (an eye disorder), as well as damage to crops and plankton (the tiny plants and animals that float in a body of water and are what fish eat). The reduction of plankton and plant life will lead to an increase in carbon dioxide levels. In fact, worldwide levels of carbon dioxide have increased by 8 percent since 1972. Although great strides have been made to control air pollution that is toxic to people and the environment, there is still a long way to go.

What to Do to Protect Against Outside Air Pollution

All the potential dangers in the air cannot be avoided, but it is important to try to limit exposure to pollutants or unhealthy levels of pollutants.

- Playing outside on days when the air quality is at an unhealthy level is not advisable (local television and radio stations generally report this).
- Homes and schools should be tested for lead-based paint.
- Lead-based paint must be properly contained or removed from homes and schools.

- Carpools can be coordinated to get to and from activities, thus cutting down on car fumes.
- People can get involved in recycling and pollution-control efforts in their communities.

INDOOR AIR POLLUTION

The quality of the air people breathe in outdoor activities is a concern, but the quality of the air indoors is an equally, possibly even more, significant issue of environmental health. Research suggests that Americans spend 90 percent of their time indoors. And, in recent years, scientific studies have revealed that the air in homes and other buildings may contain even more pollutants, or higher levels of pollutants, than the air outdoors. These severe levels of indoor air pollution have been found even in highly industrial metropolitan areas, where one might automatically assume that air pollution risks would be greater outdoors than indoors. In light of this research, organizations like the Environmental Protection Agency are taking a closer look at what's happening with air quality inside homes, schools, and offices. Some of the key threats to air quality, and in turn to human health, are discussed below.

Tobacco Smoke

Environmental tobacco smoke (ETS) is the mixture of the smoke from a lit cigarette, pipe, or cigar and the smoke exhaled by the person smoking. ETS exposure is sometimes referred to as passive smoking or secondhand smoking. Even though the affected person is not actively lighting up and inhaling, enough smoke is being breathed into the person's lungs to have a negative impact on his or her health.

ETS contains over 4,000 chemical compounds. According to the EPA, over 40 percent of these chemicals are known to cause cancer in humans or animals, and many of them are strong irritants. A 1992 EPA study (Respiratory Health Effects of Passive Smoking: Lung Cancer and Other Disorders) evaluated the risks of ETS to nonsmokers and concluded that ETS posed a significant health threat to nonsmokers, putting them at risk for a wide range of irritations and illnesses. Most significantly, the study indicated that, annually, exposure to ETS is responsible for about 3,000 lung-cancer deaths among nonsmoking adults.

The 1986 Surgeon General's Report concluded that physically separating smokers from nonsmokers in a home or office—by putting the smokers in a separate room—did not entirely eliminate a nonsmoker's exposure to ETS. Nonsmoking regulations have been put into effect in many offices and public areas to protect nonsmokers from the harmful effects of secondhand smoke. Nevertheless, individuals have to be conscientious about their exposure to ETS in private homes and unregulated public areas.

Radon

Radon is a colorless, odorless, radioactive gas produced by the naturally occurring breakdown of the chemical element uranium in soil or rocks. Radon gas is released into the air when radon is broken down. It can get into a home through dirt floors, cracks in concrete walls and floors, floor drains, and sumps (underground drainage system, or cesspool). When radon gas enters and becomes trapped in a home, it can build up to dangerous levels and pose threats to human health. In rare cases, building materials used in a home give off radon. Radon can also surface in well water.

When inhaled, high levels of radon can cause lung cancer in people. It can also be unhealthy to swallow radon-contaminated water. But the most serious exposure is from breathing air with high levels of radon. Organizations like the Centers for Disease Control and Prevention, the American Lung

Secondhand smoke is disturbing, and harmful, to nonsmokers. (Custom Medical Stock Photo. Reproduced by permission.)

REPORTED HEALTH EFFECTS OF ETS (SECONDHAND SMOKE) EXPOSURE

- There is an increased risk of lung cancer in nonsmoking adults.

- ETS endangers, or damages, the respiratory health of hundreds of thousands of children each year.

- Parents who smoke in the presence of their children increase the risk for the children to develop lower respiratory tract infections such as bronchitis.

- Infants and children exposed to ETS by smoking parents more frequently have problems with coughing, excess mucus, and wheezing.

- ETS annually causes between 150,000–300,000 lower respiratory infections in children under the age of eighteen months.

- Older children might experience reduced lung function due to ETS exposure.

- Asthmatic children are especially vulnerable to effects of ETS.

- Exposure to secondhand smoke can increase the number or severity of asthma attacks experienced by hundreds of thousands of young asthma sufferers each year.

- Each year, ETS might lead to the development of asthma in thousands of nonasthmatic children.

- The asthmatic condition of 200,000 to 1,000,000 children is worsened each year as a result of ETS exposure.

- ETS causes significant eye, ear, nose, and throat irritations.

- ETS may negatively affect cardiovascular (relating to the heart and lungs) health.

Association, and the American Medical Association agree that radon causes thousands of lung-cancer deaths each year. There is also agreement that many of these deaths could be prevented by better controls on indoor air pollution. According to estimates by the Environmental Protection Agency, on average there are about 14,000 deaths caused by radon in the United States each year. Studies also suggest that smokers are especially vulnerable to health risks posed by radon.

Stoves, Heaters, Fireplaces, and Chimneys

Harmful pollutants, in the form of gases or particles, can be released into the air by combustion (or burning) processes that take place in the home. Poorly ventilated kerosene and gas space heaters, wood stoves, fireplaces, and gas stoves can release combustion products. Other sources include improperly installed chimneys and flues and cracked furnace equipment. Fireplaces and wood stoves, in particular, can backdraft (or draw) pollutants from the chimney into a room. Carbon monoxide and nitrogen dioxide particles are generated by combustion.

Carbon Monoxide

A colorless, odorless gas, carbon monoxide makes it difficult for the body to circulate oxygen. In large amounts, carbon monoxide can lead to unconsciousness and even death. Smaller amounts result in headaches, dizziness, nausea, disorientation, and fatigue. People who suffer from heart disease might experience increased chest pain when exposed to carbon monoxide. Beside people with chronic heart diseases, the negative health effects brought on by carbon monoxide exposure particularly endanger infants and the elderly.

Nitrogen Dioxide

Like carbon monoxide, nitrogen dioxide is a gas that cannot be seen or smelled. It irritates the eyes, ears, nose, and throat. Human exposure to large quantities of nitrogen dioxide (or repeated exposure to lower quantities over a long period of time) can cause shortness of breath or lead to increased risk of respiratory infection. Some studies with animals indicate that nitrogen dioxide exposure can lead to lung diseases such as emphysema. Adults and children who suffer from asthma or other breathing disorders are especially vulnerable if exposed to nitrogen dioxide.

Cracks in basement walls are a site where radon gas might leak into the home. (Photograph by Robert J. Huffman. Field Mark Publications. Reproduced by permission.)

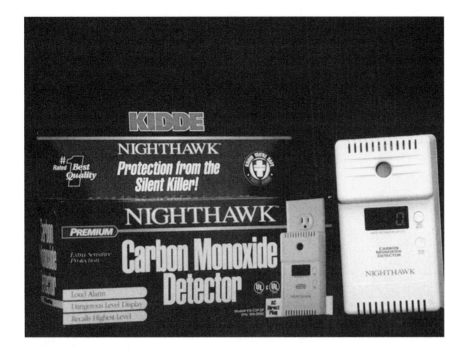

Carbon monoxide detectors are easy to install in the home and help protect families from this gas, which is colorless and odorless. (Photograph by Robert J. Huffman. Field Mark Publications. Reproduced by permission.)

Particles

Particles are released when fuel does not burn completely. They can enter and bury themselves in human lungs, where they can cause irritation or damage. Particles also provide a hanger for other airborne pollutants (such as radon, for example) to latch onto and use to gain entry into human lung tissue. Cancer-causing radon, for example, could latch onto a particle produced by incomplete combustion. The radon would be inhaled with the particle and end up lodged deep in the human lungs where it could lead to cancer.

Household Products

Many household products contain organic (carbon-containing) chemicals. These products can release polluting organic chemicals or compounds while in use or storage. Products with organic chemical ingredients include paints; varnishes; wax; many disinfecting, degreasing, or cosmetic agents; and fuels. According to the EPA, twelve common organic pollutants have been found in the air in homes at levels two to five times higher than the levels at which they were found in the air outside homes (even in industrial areas). EPA studies also indicate that people using household products, as well as others, can be exposed to high levels of chemical pollutants. These chemical pollutants also linger in the air even after the product is no longer being applied.

Healthy Living **125**

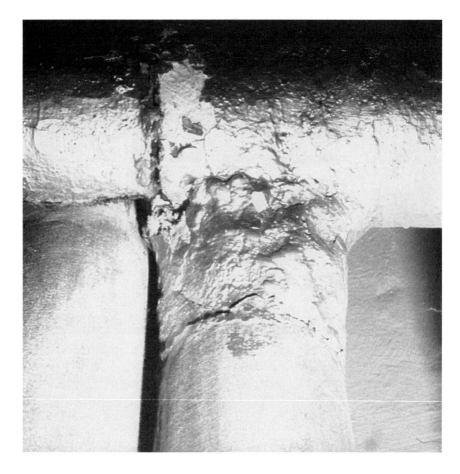

Many old buildings still contain asbestos-wrapped pipes. (Custom Medical Stock Photo. Reproduced by permission.)

Evidence is still being gathered as to the short- and long-term health risks of organic chemicals released by household products, and what concentrations or lengths of exposure are dangerous. Findings to date suggest that health risks include respiratory tract irritation, headaches, dizziness, visual disorders, and impaired memory. A larger concern is that many organic compounds have been shown to cause cancer in animals and are suspected, or proven, to be cancer-causing agents in humans. While research continues, household products should be used in well-ventilated areas and according to label instructions.

Asbestos

A mineral fiber, asbestos was frequently used to insulate or fireproof building materials until studies began to reveal asbestos-related health dangers. The EPA has banned some asbestos products and manufacturers are limiting their use of asbestos products, but some older homes and buildings built before 1978 were built with asbestos-based materials. In these buildings, asbestos can appear in pipe and furnace insulation materials, shingles, textured paints, and floor tiles.

Asbestos fibers are dangerous when airborne. They can become airborne if asbestos-containing materials are cut, sanded, or disturbed in removal or remodeling efforts. Once airborne, tiny asbestos fibers can be inhaled and accumulate in human lungs, where they can cause cancer, meso-thelioma (cancer of chest and abdominal linings), and asbestosis. Asbestosis creates scar tissue in the lungs that cannot be repaired; this can be a life-threatening condition. Asbestos-related diseases have mostly been traced to high exposure on the job, or exposure to asbestos particles carried into a home on clothing and equipment by someone working a job involving high exposure to asbestos.

Lead

Like other chemicals that pose health risks, lead cannot be seen, smelled, or tasted. Since it does not break down naturally, trained professionals must physically remove lead sources from the environment they are polluting. Be-

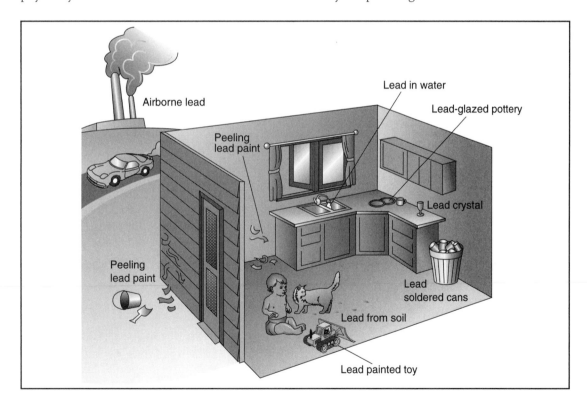

Common sources of lead exposure include lead-based paint; dust and soil; drinking water; canned food; and eating utensils, such as plates and glasses, that are lead-based. (Electronic Illustrators Group. Reproduced by permission of Gale Group.)

fore the health risks of lead were known, lead was used in paint and water pipes. Today, most house paint is almost entirely lead-free, and lead-based materials are not used in household plumbing systems. On the other hand, homes and buildings built before 1960, and even as late as 1978, may contain lead-based paint. Lead-based paint in good condition usually does not pose a risk. But lead-based paint in bad condition can cause serious problems.

Lead gets into the body from breathing contaminated lead dust from air, swallowing contaminated water, or ingesting lead-filled paint chips or soil. Problem sites can include window frames, walls, doors and doorframes, stairs, railings, banisters, and any objects or surfaces covered in lead-based paint. Hobbies such as refinishing furniture and making pottery or stained glass can produce lead remains. Workers who have jobs in construction, demolition, radiator repair, or handling batteries could carry dust from their job sites back to their homes. Soil that contains lead can also be easily tracked into the house from outdoors.

In spite of the growing awareness about the dangers of lead poisoning, the Centers for Disease Control and Prevention report that one in eleven American children has a high level of lead in their blood. Children can have especially serious health problems if they consume lead, causing learning disabilities, decreased growth, hyperactivity, and even brain damage. Pregnant women are also especially sensitive to lead-related problems.

Pesticides

Surveys have shown that at least one indoor pesticide product is used in about 75 percent of U.S. homes each year. Insecticides and disinfectants are used even more. Indoor exposure is responsible for 80 percent of an average American's exposure to pesticides, according to a recent study. The study also found that the air content of average homes could have high levels of as many as twelve different pesticides. While this research attributes 80 percent of an average American's pesticide exposure to indoor sources, actual pesticide use in the home does not accurately account for all the pesticides that are found in the air in a home. Contaminated air, water, or soil that is brought into a household from the outdoors can also contribute to the pesticide content in the home. Other contributors are stored pesticides, and household objects and surfaces where pesticides can accumulate, then later be released.

According to the 1990 records of the American Association of Poison Control Centers (AAPCC), 79,000 children were exposed to, or poisoned by, a household pesticide in that year. The AAPCC also reported that in almost 50 percent of households with children under age five, at least one pesticide product was stored in a place children could access.

When people use pesticides (insecticides, disinfectants, repellants, and rodenticides) in and around their homes, they should always keep in mind that how and where they handle, apply, and dispose of pesticides might also affect the environment and other people, pets, plants, and wildlife.

Effects of Indoor Air Pollution

There can be both short- and long-term effects from exposure to indoor air pollution. Short-term or immediate effects include irritations of the eyes, nose, and throat; headaches; dizziness; and fatigue. Symptoms of diseases such as asthma might appear not long after a single, or repeated, exposure to indoor air pollutants. Other, more serious, health problems, such as respiratory diseases, heart disease, and even cancer, may surface a long time after a person's first exposure to an indoor air pollutant (or several indoor air pollutants). These serious, even fatal, diseases might also appear after a person has been repeatedly exposed to the same air pollutants over a long period of time.

What to Do to Protect Against Indoor Air Pollution

All the pollutants can't be eliminated from the air people breathe, nor can there be an avoidance of some exposure to them. It is possible, however, to have protection against exposure to indoor air pollution, or at least against dangerous levels of indoor air pollution, by taking some basic steps:

TOBACCO SMOKE. Tobacco smoke exposure can be reduced or eliminated by:

- not smoking
- discouraging smoking in the home
- discouraging people from smoking around infants and children

RADON. Exposure to radon can be controlled by:

- being sure all living space is properly ventilated
- encouraging parents/teachers to have the air circulating at home and in school checked for radon levels and other pollutants
- having well water tested, and if necessary treated, for high levels of radon
- taking time to identify the sources of air pollution problems
- keeping windows open when painting to control, or prevent, problems
- encouraging everyone at home or at school who works on painting or soldering projects or hobbies to work carefully and clean up thoroughly
- investigating products and services to improve ventilation and clean air
- keeping living and working spaces as clean and dust-free as possible

STOVES, HEATERS, FIREPLACES, AND CHIMNEYS. Pollution from stoves, heaters, fireplaces and chimneys can be eliminated or reduced by:

- following instructions when installing and using unvented, fuel-burning space heaters
- having exhaust fans over gas cooking stoves and adjusting burners correctly

- making sure wood-stove emissions meet EPA standards
- selecting a stove that is the correct size for the space in which it will be used
- arranging the annual inspection of central air conditioning and heating systems
- repairing damaged or broken parts immediately

HOUSEHOLD PRODUCTS. With household products it is advisable to:

- read and follow label instructions
- safely dispose of chemicals that are old or no longer used
- buy household products on a need-only basis so a lot of chemicals aren't stored
- limit exposure to paint strippers, adhesive removers, and aerosol spray paints
- ask dry-cleaners to remove as much as possible of the perchloroethylene (active chemical agent used in dry-cleaning)

ASBESTOS. Because of asbestos's hazardous nature one should:

- not tamper with asbestos material that is in good condition in the home
- avoid cutting, ripping, or sanding asbestos-based materials
- have a professional contain or remove asbestos in the home

Common household chemicals can be hazardous to humans when used improperly.
(Photograph by Robert J. Huffman. Field Mark Publications. Reproduced by permission.)

LEAD. To prevent problems related to lead, it's important to:

- get tested for lead poisoning
- use a solution of water mixed with powdered dishwasher detergent to wash floors and windowsills
- be sure children are not chewing on objects or surfaces covered with lead-based paint
- get professional help to remove lead paint from the home
- have water tested for dangerous levels of lead
- run cold water for thirty to sixty seconds if it has not been used in over two hours to give pipes a chance to clear before drinking or cooking
- not store food or liquid in lead crystal or in pottery with high lead content

PESTICIDES. For protection from pesticides, it's important to:

- read and follow exactly all label instructions
- never use a large amount of a pesticide, or use it more frequently than what is indicated
- limit exposure to moth repellants
- keep living space clean and well ventilated
- avoid direct physical contact with pesticide being used
- cover exposed human/pet food and water containers before applying pesticides

ENDOCRINE DISRUPTERS

Most living animals, including human beings, have an endocrine system. The endocrine system—made up of glands such as the pituitary gland and thyroid gland—functions by releasing hormones into the bloodstream. Hormones are like packets of information, which are sent to different cells to stimulate specific reactions or processes that help to keep the body functioning properly. Some man-made chemicals look and act like these naturally-occurring hormones. These chemicals are called endocrine disrupters because, when they get into the bloodstream of a person or animal, they can prevent the real hormones from doing their jobs. Endocrine disrupters are synthetic chemicals or chemical byproducts. They are fat-soluble, which means they dissolve in fat, not water, and therefore remain in the body longer. Most endocrine disrupters come from pesticides or industrial chemicals.

What Endocrine Disrupters Do

Endocrine disrupters usually interfere with real hormones in one of three ways. They can be

WHAT DOES THE ENDOCRINE SYSTEM DO?

Body functions affected by the endocrine system in humans are:

body growth; organ development; metabolism; kidney function; body temperature; calcium regulation; blood pressure; reproductive cycles.

In addition to the above list, the following are also affected just in animals:

mating behaviors; migration; fat distribution; hibernation

mimics, blocks, or triggers. *Mimics* imitate real hormones. The mere presence of these chemical imposters disturbs the body's delicate hormonal balance. When this balance is off, the body does not function properly. *Blocks* are endocrine disrupters that actually get in the way of real hormones. Hormones have to attach to a certain part of a cell, called a receptor site, to tell the cell what it needs to do to keep a particular organ or process running smoothly. Endocrine disrupters can block this information by attaching to a receptor site so that the real hormone cannot. With the endocrine disrupter in the way, the information the cell needs to function does not get through. *Triggers* do not just imitate or block real hormones; these endocrine disrupters actually give the body directions about what it should do. When the body responds to these signals, things go wrong because, unlike the real hormones, the endocrine disrupters do not know what they should be telling the body to do. The artificial triggers cause inappropriate growth, changes in metabolism, or other abnormal interactions that can create biological chaos.

Where Endocrine Disrupters Come From?

A wide range of synthetic chemicals and chemical byproducts developed for commercial and industrial purposes are suspected of being, or producing, endocrine disrupters. Many detergents, pesticides, plastics, and varnishes, for example, are made with or from endocrine disrupter chemicals. Through production and use of these products, endocrine disrupters are released into the environment where they can pollute food and water sources. Later, these artificial, hormone-disrupting substances can get into the bloodstreams of the people or animals who consume food and water from the contaminated sources.

Endocrine disrupters do not just come from environmental pollution. They can also be contained in synthetic drugs and be absorbed into a person's bloodstream when the drug is taken.

Most Common Endocrine Disrupters

The most common endocrine disrupters are known as environmental estrogens. Examples include PCBs and Dioxin. Environmental estrogens mimic the natural estrogens (female sex hormones) and androgens (male sex hormones), which control reproduction and sexual characteristics. Environmental estrogens have their biggest impact on fetuses (infants developing in a mother's womb). Once a baby is born, their sexual features are developed, but in the womb the sex hormones play a key role in shaping an infant's sexual makeup. The presence of artificial hormones in the mother's body can interfere with, or alter, the normal course of a fetus's sexual development.

Environmental estrogens have a particularly dramatic effect on males. Exposure to environmental estrogens in the womb can lead to a male being born with an unnatural amount of female sexual characteristics, or even a hermaphroditic condition, which is when a person has both male and female sexual features.

Sexual characteristics are not the only element that environmental estrogens can affect. Other biological features—such as bones, cardiovascular system, memory, and immune system—can be weakened in a male or female baby who is exposed to environmental estrogens in the womb.

The Risks Associated with Endocrine Disrupters

Many studies conducted on animal populations in chemically contaminated areas strongly suggest that endocrine disrupters are potent and frequent pollutants of our food and water sources. Abnormalities, particularly sexual

Dead egrets on the shore of Lake Erie. (Photograph by Robert J. Huffman. Field Mark Publications. Reproduced by permission.)

DOCUMENTED EFFECTS OF ENDOCRINE DISRUPTERS

Polluted Species from the Great Lakes

The Great Lakes area is known to be a highly contaminated area, with particularly elevated levels of endocrine disrupters. Studies done on species from the Great Lakes area have revealed a range of abnormalities, such as the following:

• Low rates of egg production, abnormal enlargement of the thyroid gland, early mortal-

ity rates, and low reproduction rates have been seen in several fish species, especially salmon.

• Birds in the area (including bald eagles and herring gulls) that feed on these fish have demonstrated symptoms similar to those observed in the fish.

• Hermaphroditic fish (genetically male fish with female genitals) have been observed.

The Florida Everglades

A study of male alligators was conducted in Lake Apopka, Florida, which is situated near a now-closed chemical processing plant. DDE, a byproduct of the pesticide DDT, was generated at this plant. The male alligators in this area were found to have abnormally small penises, while male alligators in other (nonpolluted) Florida regions had normal size genitalia. Scientists attribute the Lake Apopka alligators' condition to exposure to DDE.

DES

A prescription drug called diethylstilbestrol (DES) was produced in the 1940s. The drug, which contained a synthetic estrogen compound, was administered to women who experienced complications during their pregnancies. It was later discovered to cause problems in the daughters of the women. The daughters who had had fetal exposure to the drug had depression, decreased fertility, abnormal pregnancies, organ dysfunction, and increased occurrences of cancers, especially of reproductive organs.

Microwaving food in Styrofoam or plastic containers may allow plastics in the container to leach into the food being reheated. It is best to heat foods on microwave-safe dishware. (Photograph by Robert J. Huffman. Field Mark Publications. Reproduced by permission.)

abnormalities, have been observed in the offspring of the animals that live, feed, and drink in these contaminated areas. Although similar studies have not been undertaken in human populations, many scientists are concerned that the risks of human exposure to endocrine disrupters might be significant.

Pesticides can get into food supplies directly or indirectly. They can be sprayed on crops, which people later consume. Industrial pollution releases endocrine disrupters into the environment, exposing fish, cattle, hogs, and poultry. If the fish and animals ingest the chemicals, they will be contained in their fat and later passed on to human consumers.

Scientists have also expressed concern about plastics and artificial materials used in food preparation and storage. They are concerned that a leaching process might take place. Leaching is when dangerous products found in plastics move from the plastics into the food in the container. Although it is in the early stages, recent research has shown that endocrine disrupters can leach out of plastic containers into the liquid they are holding. Similar concerns have been raised about tin cans. Research suggests that the coating a tin can is treated with might contain endocrine disrupter chemicals, which are able to leach into the can's contents.

A sampling of common foods made with pesticide-free, organically-grown ingredients. (Photograph by Robert J. Huffman. Field Mark Publications. Reproduced by permission.)

Incinerators and other equipment that use combustion release endocrine disrupters into the atmosphere. Once released into the atmosphere, they pose a risk to human life and wildlife.

Drinking water sources must also be monitored carefully. Contaminated drinking water could also expose humans to endocrine disrupters.

The effects of exposure to endocrine disrupters are not always immediate. It may take awhile for symptoms to surface, or the effects and problems could show up in the next generation (meaning in the children of the person who was exposed).

What Can Be Done to Protect Against Endocrine Disrupters

The scientific community is pursuing research in the area of endocrine disrupters. Environmental groups like the World Wildlife Foundation are encouraging the government to crack down on industry's use of chemicals that are proven (or suspected) to be endocrine disrupters. And more testing needs to be done to determine other chemicals that are endocrine disrupters. While investigation and regulation of endocrine disrupters is taking place on a national scale, people can protect and educate themselves on an individual level, too. Some suggestions for limiting exposure to endocrine disrupters are to:

- limit fat and oil intake (since endocrine disrupters tend to accumulate in fats)
- avoid cooking, microwaving, and storing food in plastic or styrofoam containers
- use pesticide-free, organically-grown foods
- not handle pesticides
- investigate the origin of fish, poultry, and meat by asking the grocery store manager what the source is
- encourage local store owners and managers to purchase produce and animal-based products from waters, farms, and rangelands that have been tested for pollution and contamination
- get involved in antipollution efforts in your community
- write to state legislators to find out their views on key statewide environmental issues

THE BLACK PLAGUE

Environmental health has been an issue since ancient times. Even in the earliest days of civilization, it became clear that infections could be produced and spread in certain environments. Bubonic plague, nicknamed "the Black Plague," which claimed 25 million lives in Europe from 1347 to 1532, is an example of an infectious disease made worse by environmental conditions. Unsanitary living conditions gave the fleas and rats that carried the disease access to homes, bedding, and food. As people realized how important the proper management of drinking water, food supplies, and sewage was, new methods were developed to combat contamination and pollution. In modern society, health problems are now more commonly thought to be lifestyle-related, rather than correlated to environmental causes. But health risks from the environment can be substantial even in a sophisticated, technologically advanced society. In fact, many of the modern processes and products themselves are responsible for creating a whole new range of environmental risks to be explored and controlled.

FOR MORE INFORMATION

Books

Dolan, Edward F. *Our Poisoned Waters*. New York: Cobblehill, 1997.

Kahl, Jonathan D.W. *Hazy Skies: Weather and the Environment*. Minneapolis, Minn.: Lerner Publications, 1997.

Willis, Terri and Wallace B. Black. *Cars: An Environmental Challenge*. New York: Children's Press, 1992.

Wright, David. *Facts on File Environmental Atlas*. New York: Facts on File, 1998.

Young, Lisa. *Pesticides*. New York: Lucent Books, 1995.

Zike, Dinah. *Earth Science Book: Activities for Kids*. New York: John Wiley and Sons, 1993.

Zonderman, Jon. *Environmental Diseases (Bodies in Crises)*. New York: Twenty-First Century Books, 1995.

Web sites

Children's Environmental Health Network. [Online] http://www.cehn.org (Accessed August 19, 1999)

Earthforce. [Online] http://www.earthforce.org (Accessed August 19, 1999)

Environmental Health Coalition. [Online] http://www.environmentalhealth.org (Accessed August 19, 1999)

The Environmental Protection Agency's (EPA) site for students. [Online] http:// www.epa.gov/students (Accessed August 19, 1999)

National Education Association Health Information Network. [Online] http:// www.nea.org (Accessed August 19, 1999)

Bibliography

BOOKS

General

Adderholt-Elliot, Miriam and Jan Goldberg. *Perfectionism: What's Bad About Being Too Good.* Minneapolis, MN: Free Spirit Publishing, 1999.

Davitz, Lois Jean, Joel R. Davitz, Lois Leiderman Davitz, and Jo Davitz. *20 Tough Questions Teenagers Ask: And 20 Tough Answers.* Minneapolis, MN: Paulist Press, 1998.

Holm, Sharon Lane (Illustrator) and Faith Hickman Brynie. *101 Questions Your Brain Has Asked About Itself but Couldn't Answer. . .Until Now.* Brookfield, CT: Millbrook Press, 1998.

Kalergis, Mary Motley. *Seen and Heard: Teenagers Talk About Their Lives.* New York: Stewart Tabori & Chang, 1998.

McCoy, Ph.D., Kathy, and Charles Wibbelsman, M.D.(Contributor). *Life Happens: A Teenager's Guide to Friends, Failure, Sexuality, Love, Rejection, Addiction, Peer Pressure, Families, Loss, Depression, Change and Other Challenges of Living.* Perigee Paperbacks, 1996.

Parsley, Bonnie M., Scott Peck. *The Choice Is Yours: A Teenager's Guide to Self Discovery, Relationships, Values, and Spiritual Growth.* New York: Fireside, 1992.

Roehm, Michelle (Editor) and Marci Doane Roth (Illustrator). *Girls Know Best: Advice for Girls from Girls on Just About Everything.* Beyond Words Pub. Co., 1997.

Roehm, Michelle (Editor) and Marianne Monson-Burton (Editor). *Boys Know It All: Wise Thoughts and Wacky Ideas From Guys Just Like You.* Beyond Words Pub. Co., 1998.

Turner, Priscilla (Editor), and Susan Pohlmann (Editor). *A Boy's Guide to Life: The Complete Instructions.* New York: Penguin USA, 1997.

Eating Disorders

Chiu, Christina. *Eating Disorder Survivors Tell Their Stories.* (The Teen Health Library of Eating Disorder Prevention). Minneapolis, MN: Hazelden Information Education, 1999.

Davis, Brangien. *What's Real, What's Ideal: Overcoming a Negative Body Image.* (The Teen Health Library of Eating Disorder Prevention). Minneapolis, MN: Hazelden Information Education, 1999.

Erlanger, Ellen. *Eating Disorders: A Question and Answer Book About Anorexia Nervosa and Bulima Nervosa.* Minneapolis, MN: Lerner Publications Company, 1988.

Frissell, Susan and Paula Harney. *Eating Disorders and Weight Control.* (Issues in Focus). Springfield, NJ: Enslow Publishers, Inc., 1998.

Harmon, Dan and Carol C. Nadelson. *Anorexia Nervosa: Starving for Attention.* (Encyclopedia of Psychological Disorders). New York: Chelsea House Publishers, 1998.

Kaminker, Laura. *Exercise Addiction: When Fitness Becomes an Obsession.* (The Teen Health Library of Eating Disorder Prevention). Minneapolis, MN: Hazelden Information Education, 1999.

Kolodny, Nancy J. *When Food's a Foe: How You Can Confront and Conquer Your Eating Disorder.* Boston, MA: Little Brown & Co., 1998.

Moe, Barbara. *Understanding the Causes of a Negative Body Image.* Hazelden Information Education. Minneapolis, MN: Hazelden Information Education, 1999.

Monroe, Judy. *Understanding Weight-Loss Programs: A Teen Eating Disorder Prevention Book.* Minneapolis, MN: Hazelden Information Education, 1999.

Patterson, Charles. *Eating Disorders (Teen Hot Line).* Chatham, NJ: Raintree/Steck Vaughn, 1995.

Smith, Erica. *Anorexia Nervosa: When Food is the Enemy.* Minneapolis, MN: Hazelden Information Education, 1999.

Sneddon, Pamela Shires. *Body Image: A Reality Check.* (Issues in Focus.) Springfield, NJ: Enslow Publishers, Inc., 1999.

Stanley, Debbie. *Understanding Anorexia Nervosa.* Minneapolis, MN: Hazelden Information Education, 1999.

Stanley, Debbie. *Understanding Bulimia Nervosa.* Minneapolis, MN: Hazelden Information Education, 1999.

Habits and Behaviors

Connelly, Elizabeth Russell, Beth Connolly, and Carol C. Nadelson. *Through a Glass Darkly: The Psychological Effects of Marijuana and Hashish.* (Encylopedia of Psychological Disorders). New York: Chelsea House Publishers, 1999.

Holmes, Ann, Carol C. Nadelson (Editor), and Claire E. Reinburg (Editor). *Cutting the Pain Away: Understanding Self-Mutilation.* (Encyclopedia of Psychological Disorders). New York: Chelsea House Publishers, 1999.

Klein, Wendy. *Drugs and Denial.* (Drug Abuse Prevention Library). New York: The Rosen Publishing Group, 1998.

Peacock, Nancy, Carol C. Nadelson (Editor), and Claire E. Reinburg. *Drowning Our Sorrows: Psychological Effects of Alcohol Abuse.* New York: Chelsea House Publishers, 1999.

Snyder, Solomon H. (Editor) and P. Mick Richardson. *Flowering Plants: Magic in Bloom.* (Encyclopedia of Psychoactive Drugs, Series 1.) New York: Chelsea House Publishers, 1992.

Wilkinson, Beth. *Drugs and Depression.* Minneapolis, MN: Hazelden Information Education, 1997.

Mental Health

Adler, Joe Ann. *Stress: Just Chill Out!* (Teen Issues). Springfield, NJ: Enslow Publishers, 1997.

Barrett, Susan L., Pamela Espeland (Editor), and J. Urbanovic (Translator). *It's All in Your Head: A Guide to Understanding Your Brain and Boosting Your Brain Power.* Minneapolis, MN: Free Spirit Publishing, 1992.

Carlson, Dale Bick, Carol Nicklaus (Illustrator), and R. E. Mark Lee. *Stop the Pain: Teen Meditations.* Madison, CT: Bick Pub House, 1999.

Carlson, Dale Bick, Hannah Carlson, and Carol Nicklaus (Illustrator). *Where's Your Head?: Psychology for Teenagers.* Madison, CT: Bick Publishing House, 1998.

Espeland, Pamela and Elizabeth Verdick. *Making Every Day Count: Daily Readings for Young People on Solving Problems, Setting Goals, and Feeling Good About Yourself.* Minneapolis, MN: Free Spirit Publishing, 1998.

Hipp, Earl, Pamela Espeland, and Michael Fleishman (Illustrator). *Fighting Invisible Tigers: A Stress Management Guide for Teens.* Minneapolis, MN: Free Spirit Publishing, 1995.

Kincher, Jonni and Pamela Espeland (Editor). *Psychology for Kids II: 40 Fun Experiments That Help You Learn About Others.* Minneapolis, MN: Free Spirit Publishing, 1998.

Kincher, Jonni, Bach, Julie S. (Editor), and Steve Michaels (Illustrator). *Psychology for Kids: 40 Fun Tests That Help You Learn About Yourself.* Minneapolis, MN: Free Spirit Publishing, 1995.

Krulik, Nancy E. *Don't Stress! How To Keep Life's Problems Little.* New York: Scholastic Trade, 1998.

Miller, Shannon (Introduction), Nancy Ann Richardson (Contributor). *Winning Every Day: Gold Medal Advice for a Happy, Healthy Life!* New York: Bantam Doubleday Dell, 1998.

Packard, Gwen K. *Coping With Stress.* Minneapolis, MN: Hazelden Information Education, 1997.

Policoff, Stephen Phillip. *The Dreamer's Companion: A Young Person's Guide to Understanding Dreams and Using Them Creatively.* Chicago: Chicago Review Press, 1997.

Romain, Trevor and Elizabeth Verdick. *What on Earth Do You Do When Someone Dies?* Minneapolis, MN: Free Spirit Publishing, 1999.

Mental Illness

Connelly, Elizabeth Russell and Carol C. Nadelson. *Conduct Unbecoming: Hyperactivity, Attention Deficit, and Disruptive Behavior Disorders.* (Encyclopedia of Psychological Disorders). New York: Chelsea House Publishers, 1998.

Garland, E. Jane. *Depression Is the Pits, But I'm Getting Better: A Guide for Adolescents.* Washington, D.C.: Magination Press, 1998.

Gellman, Marc, Thomas Hartman, and Deborah Tilley (Illustrator). *Lost and Found: A Kid's Book for Living Through Loss.* New York: Morrow Junior, 1999.

Holmes, Ann, Dan Harmon, and Carol C. Nadelson (Editor). *The Tortured Mind: The Many Faces of Manic Depression.* (Encyclopedia of Psychological Disorders). New York: Chelsea House Publishers, 1998.

Kaminker, Laura. *Exercise Addiction: When Fitness Becomes an Obsession.* (The Teen Health Library of Eating Disorder Prevention). Minneapolis, MN: Hazelden Information Education, 1999.

Moe, Barbara. *Understanding the Causes of a Negative Body Image.* Minneapolis, MN: Hazelden Information Education, 1999.

Monroe, Judy. *Phobias: Everything You Wanted to Know, but Were Afraid to Ask.* (Issues in Focus). Springfield, NJ: Enslow Publishers, Inc., 1996.

Nardo, Don. *Anxiety and Phobias.* (Encyclopedia of Psychological Disorders). New York: Chelsea House Publishers, 1992.

Porterfield, Kay Marie. *Straight Talk About Post-Traumatic Stress Disorder: Coping With the Aftermath of Trauma.* Checkmark Books, 1996.

Silverstein, Alvin, Virginia Silverstein, and Laura Silverstein Nunn. *Depression.* (Diseases and People.) Springfield, NJ: Enslow Publishers, Inc., 1997.

Wilkinson, Beth. *Drugs and Depression.* Minneapolis, MN: Hazelden Information Education, 1997.

Sexuality

Baer, Judy. *Dear Judy, Did You Ever Like a Boy (Who Didn't Like You?).* Minneapolis, MN: Bethany House, 1993.

Basso, Michael J. *The Underground Guide to Teenage Sexuality: An Essential Handbook for Today's Teens & Parents.* Minneapolis, MN: Fairview Press, 1997.

Carlson, Dale Bick, Hannah Carlson, and Carol Nicklaus (Illustrator). *Girls Are Equal Too: How to Survive Guide for Teenage Girls.* Madison, CT: Bick Pub House, 1998.

Fenwick, Elizabeth and Robert Walker. *How Sex Works: A Clear, Comprehensive Guide for Teenagers to Emotional, Physical, and Sexual Maturity.* DK Publishing, 1994.

Gravelle, Karen, Nick Castro (Contributor), Chava Castro, and Robert Leighton (Illustrator). *What's Going on Down There: Answers to Questions Boys Find Hard to Ask.* New York: Walker & Co., 1998.

Harris, Robie H. *It's Perfectly Normal: Changing Bodies, Growing Up, Sex, and Sexual Health.* Candlewick Press, 1994.

Pogany, Susan Browning. *Sex Smart: 501 Reasons to Hold Off on Sex.* Minneapolis, MN: Fairview Press, 1998.

WEB SITES

ADOL: Adolescence Directory On-Line. http://education.indiana.edu/cas/adol/adol.html

The American Dietetic Association. http://www.eatright.org

Better Health. http://www.betterhealth.com

Centers for Disease Control and Prevention. http://www.cdc.com

Channel One. http://channelone.com/

The Children's Health Center. http://www.mediconsult.com/mc/mcsite.nsf/conditionnav/kids~sectionintroduction

Club Drugs (National Institute on Drug Abuse). http://www.clubdrugs.org

CyberDiet. http://www/cyberdiet.com

Drug-Free Resource Net (Partnership for a Drug-Free America). http://drugfreeamerica.org

bibliography

Healthfinder. http://www.healthfinder.gov

InteliHealth: Home to Johns Hopkins Health Information. http://www.intelihealth.com

Mayo Clinic Health Oasis. http://mayohealth.org

On Health. http://www.onhealth.com

Prevention Online (National Clearinghouse for Alcohol and Drug Information). http://www.health.org

The Vegetarian Resource Group. http://www.vrg.org

Index

Italic type indicates volume number; **boldface** type indicates main entries and their page numbers; (ill.) indicates photos and illustrations.

A

AA. *See* Alcoholics Anonymous
AAPCC. *See* American Association of Poison Control Centers
ABMS. *See* American Board of Medical Specialists
Abnormalities, from endocrine disrupters *1:* 133–34
Abortion *1:* 77–78
Abscess
    defined *1:* 32
    tooth *1:* 44
Abstinence. *See* Sexual abstinence
Abstract thinking, Alzheimer's disease and *3:* 311
Abuse
    sexual (*See* Sexual abuse)
    substance (*See* Substance abuse)
Accidents, sleep deprivation and *2:* 216
Accreditation, defined *2:* 166
Acetaminophen *2:* 244
    defined *2:* 240
Acetylsalicylic acid. *See* Aspirin
Acid (Drug). *See* LSD (Drug)
Acid rain *1:* 119–20
    defined *1:* 112
Acne
    medication for *2:* 240–42
    in puberty *1:* 34–36, 36 (ill.)
Acquaintance rape. *See* Date rape
Acquired immunodeficiency syndrome. *See* AIDS

Acrophobia *3:* 344 (ill.), 345
Activity, physical. *See* Physical activity
Actors and actresses, substance abuse and *3:* 385
Acupoints *2:* 279, 280 (ill.), 281, 282
Acupressure *2:* 281, 285, 286. *See also* Massage therapy
Acupuncture *2:* 167 (ill.), 279–82, 280 (ill.), 282 (ill.), 282 (ill.), 283
    defined *2:* 270
    history of *2:* 281
    managed care and *2:* 160, 160 (ill.)
    naturopathy and *2:* 276
    in recovery from drug addiction *3:* 401
Acupuncture points. *See* Acupoints
Acupuncturists *2:* 165–68, 167 (ill.)
Adaptive behavior, defined *3:* 324
ADD. *See* Attention-deficit disorder
Addams, Jane *2:* 199
Addiction *3:* 381–83
    defined *3:* 382
    to exercise (*See* Exercise addiction)
ADHD. *See* Attention-deficit/hyperactivity disorder
Adler, Alfred *3:* 416–17
Adlerian psychology *3:* 416–17
Adolescence. *See also* Puberty
    breakfast and *1:* 27–28
    calcium and *1:* 10
    dating in *1:* 69–70
    eating during *1:* 24, 28
    nicotine in *3:* 397–98
    nutrients and *1:* 3–4, 7